Hiking
the
Monadnock Region

**30 Nature Walks and Day-Hikes
in the Heart of New England**
by
Joe Adamowicz

**Second Edition, Revised & Expanded
New England Cartographics
2000**

Cover design by Bruce Scofield
Cover photos: Bruce Scofield

Text and photographs by Joe Adamowicz
Additional photographs where noted
Maps by Darrell J. King using *TOPO!* software
Text editing, typesetting, and layout by Valerie Vaughan

Publishers Cataloging in Publication

Adamowicz, Joe
   Hiking the Monadnock region : 30 nature walks and day-hikes in the heart of New England / Joe Adamowicz / edited by Valerie Vaughan-- 2nd ed., revised
   224 p. Includes maps and references.
   ISBN 1-889787-07-8
   1. Hiking--Guidebooks. 2. New Hampshire--Guidebooks.
   3. Monadnock region, New Hampshire--Hiking.
   4. Trails--New Hampshire--Guidebooks.
   I. Vaughan, Valerie
   917.4   **99-69843**

> # Due to changes in conditions, the use of information in this book is at the sole risk of the user.

Printed in the United States of America
10, 9, 8, 7, 6, 5, 4, 3, 2, 1

00 01 02 03 04 05

Preface

I first became interested in hiking the Monadnock Region while poking around the backroads in my 1970 Chevrolet Impala. Hills would suddenly come into view as surprises, then just as suddenly would disappear as the road twisted around the next turn. One day I decided to explore a few of those mysterious green bumps on foot.

Maybe it was on Gap Mountain in the soft rain when I first discovered the gentleness of this region, or perhaps I found it watching cloud filaments drift over toy villages before evaporating into a deep blue sky. I don't know exactly, but there is an intimacy here among the distant white steepled churches and long forgotten stone walls that you won't find on the frost-fractured summits of Mount Washington or Lafayette. Neither will you find peak baggers nor people in a hurry. What I think you will discover, however, is a greater appreciation for nature.

Acknowledgments

Thanks to the following people:

Debra DeCelle, Robin Chouiniere, Gene Chouiniere, Brenda Clarke, Kathleen Flammia, Kathy Cleveland, Ben Haubrich, Helen Van Ham, Bruce Scofield, Michael Walsh, Jim Bearce, George Johnson, Dwayne Denehy, Bob Spoerl, Jonathan Nute, Stephen Walker, Marshall Davenson, Valerie Vaughan, Chris Ryan, Jessie Salisbury, Bob Saudelli, Ralph Crowell, Dick Jenkins, Jay Hewett, Ted Bonner, Danny Wheeler, Brian Woodbury.

Contents

HIKE #

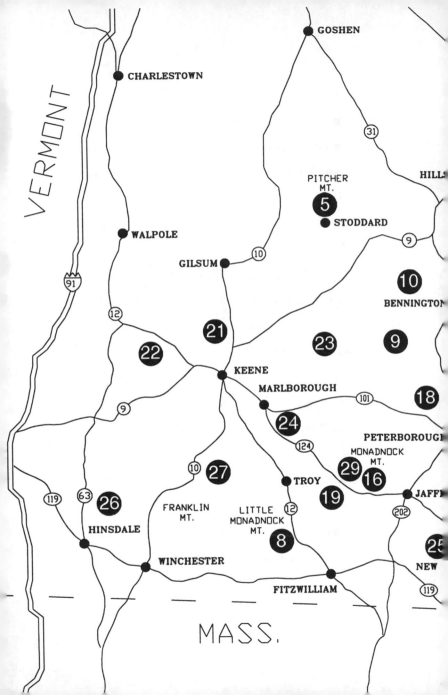

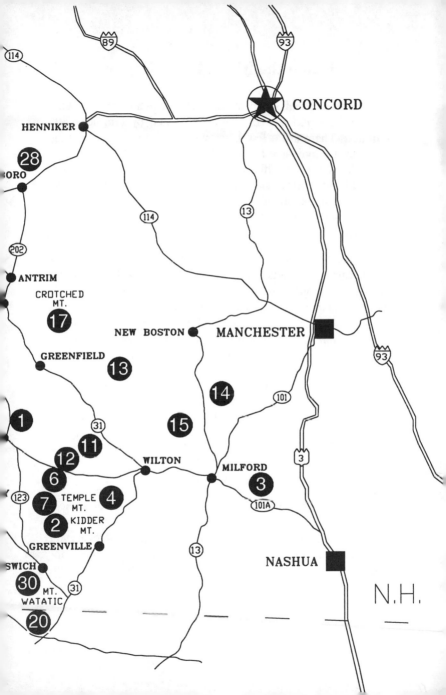

Hiking the Monadnock Region

This book is about small mountains and gentle hills, places for the most part that can be easily hiked by families with children. There are a few hikes which are more challenging and they are indicated as such. Some of the hikes in this book will take you to wildlife sanctuaries where you're apt to see a graceful blue heron stalking its dinner or a broad winged hawk with its fantail soaring slowly above a craggy mountain peak. Other hikes explore kettle holes, ponds, hemlock forests, waterfalls, or old cellar holes on roads long abandoned.

The trails are well blazed in paint on trees or rocks or with stone cairns or signs, and they are maintained by various local and regional environmental groups such as *The Friends of the Wapack, Harris Center for Conservation Education, Trailwrights, Audubon Society of New Hampshire*, and the *Appalachian Mountain Club*. Highest and lowest elevations are also given, and each trail description begins with an approximate distance and time (round trip). The routes return you to your starting point via a loop or by following the same trail in reverse. As with all hikes, keep in mind that you'll want to allow extra time for rest, lunch, poking around an old cellar hole, watching birds, identifying plants, and of course, admiring the views.

Preparations for Hiking

Before you hit the trail, here are some basic rules of advice: First and foremost, always be mindful of the risks of the outdoors. Getting lost is a potential danger wherever you hike, even on the lower elevations of southern New Hampshire. Plan your hike before you set out, with a good map showing the direction that leads to the nearest road in the event you do become lost.

If you ever get lost, sit down to rest, calm down, and figure out your location. Back up to relocate your last trail sign. If you still can't figure out your location, generally the shortest way out is toward any road, building, smoke, vehicle noise, or other signs of "civilization." Walls and fences generally lead somewhere, and although this may be only to an abandoned farm, it is probable that an old path will lead from there to a road. Natural signs show direction: vegetation tends to be larger and more open on northern slopes, smaller and denser on southern slopes. Following waterways downstream also leads toward settlements.

Another option is to try to find an identifiable landmark by climbing to the highest elevation in the immediate area. Lakes, mountains, roads and towns can be seen from above. If any of these methods fail, establish a home base. The worst thing you can do is wander blindly in any direction. Remember, if you gave prior notice to someone of your hiking plans, searchers will know where to come looking for you.

Get some basic experience in map and compass reading. The maps in this book are adequate illustrations, but learning how to read a topographic map will improve your hiking enjoyment and safety. Depending on a GPS unit or cellular phone to call for help is not a substitute for being prepared before you set out. Never put your complete faith in something that runs on batteries (batteries die and chips fail). Rely on a map, compass and common sense. You can purchase topographic maps at outdoors stores or you can order USGS maps through the government by contacting *U.S.G.S Information Services, Box 25286, Denver, Colorado 80225 (1-888-ASK-USGS; www.usgs.gov)*. Ask for a state index and price list for New Hampshire and the pamphlet describing how to read maps.

Respect the weather. Conditions can change at a moment's notice, especially here in New England when the seasons are in transition. Whenever there is doubt that the weather is changing for the worst, it is best to turn back rather than risk uncertainty. The spring is a great time to visit a waterfall and see wildflowers, but be careful of trails with stream crossings and be prepared for mud.

Many people prefer to hike in the cooler days of autumn when the air has been cleansed of the heavy haze and pesky insects, and trails are illuminated by the brilliant colors of the forest canopy. But remember, falling leaves on the trail can make it difficult to follow, and November brings with it the hunting season, so wear something orange. Prior to embarking on your trip, notify someone of your destination and the time you plan to return. Be aware of when the sun will set. If you are with a group, stay together and do not leave the marked trail or "bushwhack" for short cuts. Walk only as fast as the slowest member of your party. Consider joining a hiking organization. The Audubon Society and the Appalachian Mountain Club (AMC) sponsor a series of programs and events through regional chapters.

For even the most innocuous of hikes, wear a good pair of boots with ankle support and sturdy non-slip soles. Although tennis shoes are tempting and adequate for many of these walks, it is too easy to turn an ankle and the chance isn't worth taking. A pair of lightweight boots weigh less than three pounds and are generally made of a combination of leather and a breathable fabric. You're less likely to get blisters wearing lightweights, but they take forever to dry and don't provide much ankle support. Don't forget to bring a pair of thick socks. Shorts and T-shirt are acceptable for summer hikes, but carry a windbreaker or light jacket in case of foul weather. For late fall or early spring hiking, jackets, sweaters, and knitted hats and gloves are the order of the day.

Think in terms of layering and loose fitting. Layered clothing allows you to adjust what you are wearing to suit the temperature conditions. In cold weather wear polypropylene or lightweight wool next to the skin, and wool layers or synthetic pile over your undergarments as an insulating layer with a waterproof and windproof layer on the outside. Wearing an outer layer of nylon or breathable fabric such as GORE TEX is a good idea, especially if there is exposure to wind, which will rob your body of heat through convection. Cotton or polyester clothing can be very uncomfortable when wet and can lead to the cooling and lowering of body temperature, which in turn leads to hypothermia. Polypropylene wicks away moisture in the form of perspiration from the skin and keeps you warm. You dehydrate more easily in cold weather, so drink as much water as you would on a hot day.

Some recommended items to take along, in addition to a map and compass, include a good daypack to carry everything, extra pair of socks to keep your feet happy (socks can also double as mittens), and plenty of water (two quarts per person for longer hikes -- drink often to stay hydrated). If you are hiking under the hot sun, take extra water so you can drink six ounces every 15-to-30 minutes.

Other items to bring are waterproof matches, insect repellent, pocketknife, ribbon to mark trail intersections if you feel uncertain about the path, rainshell, hat to protect you from the sun, field guide, whistle in case you become separated, tissues or toilet paper (kept dry in a ziplock bag), sunscreen, sunglasses, first aid kit, and a small flash-light with extra batteries. Keep a small plastic bag in your back pack to carry litter home. If nature calls, find a location at least 200 feet from any water source and the trail. Dig a 4"x4" cathole for human waste; fill and cover with dirt when done. Seal used toilet paper in a plastic bag and pack it out.

Bring high energy snacks, food that's high in carbohydrates (raisins, crackers, apples, chocolate, nutrition bars, cheese, trail mix, dried fruit). Avoid diuretic foods such as coffee and soda with caffeine or sugar which cause your body to lose water and nutrients. A non-digital watch can be used as an emergency compass by pointing the hour hand toward the sun. (South will lie in the middle of the angle formed by the hour hand and the numeral 12 on the face of the watch. North will be at the point opposite it.) Other items that will enhance your hiking experience are binoculars, altimeter, camera, notepad and pen.

A word about hiking with dogs -- Many people wouldn't think of hiking without their faithful companion. But some dogs will (quite naturally) chase wildlife, defecate on the trail, scare other hikers, or otherwise get into trouble. So it's best to find out about an area before bringing along Rover. *(Dogs are not permitted on Mount Monadnock.)* If you do take your dog hiking, insure his safety and health by providing adequate water. Be aware that rough footing can cause paw injuries. And keep constant track of the whereabouts of your dog.

Hiking with Children

If you're hiking with youngsters, take advantage of their natural curiosity by providing opportunities to satisfy their imaginations. You might suggest that they keep a notebook illustrated with sketches of plant characteristics such as color, arrangement of flowers, and the number and shapes of leaves. First-hand written observation will help children build on their own experience better than trying to keep what they see in their heads. You'll be surprised at how your children's observation skills will improve.

Mt. Monadnock from Gap Mountain

When hiking with children, don't be over-ambitious in your itinerary. Be flexible and allow them time to explore. Choose an appropriate hike with achievable goals, and set a pace that is comfortable for everyone. Remember, a hike is not a race. Plan frequent stops for resting and snacking. Even young children can carry their own packs. Older children can follow the hike on a map or chart directions with a compass. With young children, gaining the summit is not as important as having fun. Children under five can walk on their own for about an hour or less. It is natural for young children to walk a short distance and then stop to explore. Hiking with children helps us rediscover spontaneity, inventiveness and wonder. Plan an interesting destination such as a waterfall, pond, stream or wildlife viewing area. Getting wet while exploring is inevitable, so bringing along a change of clothes is a good idea.

If you are bringing baby, select a specially designed child carrier that has good head and neck support, secure safety straps, a storage compartment, and feels comfortable on your back. Bring along extra diaper, towelettes, bottle, and a waterproof bag to carry out soiled diapers.

View of Mount Monadnock from the trail to Stony Top

The Geological and Cultural History
of the Monadnock Region

Located in the quiet corner of southwestern New Hampshire, the Monadnock Region is a gently rolling land of wooded hills, old country roads, and sparkling lakes, with mountain laurel that blooms on roadside slopes in late May and June. The area roughly stretches from Hinsdale, Chesterfield, and Westmoreland, along the Connecticut River on the west to Milford and Wilton on the upper reaches of the Souhegan River Valley to the east. It's bounded to the north by the hill towns of Antrim, Hillsborough, and Deering, and on the south by Rindge and New Ipswich along the Massachusetts border. Two of the hikes -- Joe English Reservation (**Hike #14**) and Ponemah Bog (**Hike #3**)-- are located in Amherst, New Hampshire, a town considered by most people to be located just outside the region. The walks are close enough in location and in spirit, however, so they are included here.

The Monadnock Region is old in terms of settlement. Most of the towns date back to the mid-1700s and have attractive, quiet village greens, white clapboarded buildings, photogenic churches and meetinghouses, and well-kept historic homes you'll want to visit before or after you complete your hike. In spite of the gravelly till spread throughout the land by the glaciers, agriculture played an important role in the formation of these communities, and swift-moving streams once powered a variety of small mills.

In the early days, a primeval forest of pine stretched from the river valleys to Canada, and lumbering was an important industry for more than a century. Brick, glass, furniture making, leather tanning, and quarrying for soapstone and granite also contributed to the early economies. Between 1790 and 1866, the Monadnock region had several glass factories, including glassworks in Lyndeborough, Temple, Stoddard, and Keene. With the development of water power, paper, textile, and other manufacturing industries flourished on the banks of the region's rivers.

Beginning in the mid-1800s, many farmers left their rocky plots of land for the deep, fertile soil of the west. The pastureland, once dotted with sheep and cattle, began retreating to forest. Today, old stone walls hidden deep in the woods are the only evidence of the people who once cleared the land, and vestiges of the mill history can be found in the dams and brick buildings along the Contoocook, Ashuelot, and Souhegan Rivers.

The development of the railroad in the mid-1800s gave an economic boost to tourism, and the towns surrounding Mount Monadnock drew summer visitors from New York, Boston, and Hartford. Lodging for visitors was provided by resort hotels, private homes, boardinghouses, inns and farmhouses.

Geologically, the Monadnock region is classified as an upland, a landscape of wooded rolling hills, ponds, lakes, and low mountains whose surface elevation ranges from 700 to 1400 feet above sea level. Above this level, a few solitary hills stand like islands overlooking the sea, enduring remnants of ancient mountains whose fortunate locations far away from main streams enabled them to survive erosional forces better than the surrounding rock. The most famous of these island hills is, of course, Mount Monadnock, the imperial example that gives the region its name. ("Monadnock" is now the term which is used by geologists for any such isolated remnant mountain.)

Mount Monadnock is like a kindly grandfather watching over the hills, villages, and towns in his broad shadow with an ever-vigilant eye. It is impossible to drive for any distance in the region without glimpsing Monadnock -- its craggy peak and long northern ridge rising above the forest on the opposite shore of Dublin Lake, poking above the ring of hills encircling the ancient glacial valley of Keene, or etched in a slate blue-gray pyramid against the sky as you round the curve beyond the Temple Mountain at Peterborough Gap on Route 101 and descend into the Contoocook River Valley.

The bedrock foundation of the ancient hills of this region is made up of metamorphosed rock which is the result of uplifting and folding from the pressurized forces deep within the earth that began more than two million years ago. This was followed by another period in which the land rose and was sculpted and scoured by vast sheets of ice advancing and retreating from the north. Meltwater streams carried away thousands of cubic feet of rock material, sand, clay, and silt, while boulders gathered up by the moving ice were strewn nearly everywhere. Geologists refer to such boulders as "glacial erratics."

The springs, swamps, bogs, lakes, and ponds were also the result of the glaciers' handiwork, making the region an ideal summer vacationland with opportunities to canoe, camp, pick blueberries, bicycle, fish, ride horseback, hunt, picnic, or visit a covered bridge, a small museum, or the annual and seasonal fairs and events. Despite its location, only 30 miles west of the urban sprawl of southern New Hampshire, the Monadnock Region remains largely unspoiled and it is a premiere area for wildlife. Moose, bear, deer, fox, fisher, coyote, and bobcat can all be seen here.

Major Hiking Trails of the Monadnock Region

A number of the day hikes in this book are located on well-known footpaths that traverse the region. The 160 mile-long *Metacomet-Monadnock Trail* begins in the Hanging Hills at Meriden, Connecticut, and continues along the traprock ridge bordering the Connecticut River and over Mount Tom, the Holyoke Range, and the Northfield Hills in Massachusetts before entering New Hampshire at the wooded town of Richmond. The M-M Trail crosses New Hampshire Route 119 to continue northward on old roads, then ascends Little Monadnock Mountain (**Hike #8**) and Gap Mountain (**Hike #19**) before terminating on the summit of Mount Monadnock.

Mount Watatic in Ashburnham, Massachusetts, marks the beginning of the *Wapack Trail* -- the oldest interstate hiking trail in the Northeast. Originally used to drive cattle from Massachusetts to the then pastured slopes of the Wapack Range, the footpath was blazed out in the 1920s and follows a long ridge along the eastern edge of the Monadnock Region. For many years the trail went through a period of neglect but has enjoyed a revival in popularity, thanks in large part to the *Friends of the Wapack* -- volunteers who maintain, blaze (yellow triangles), and clear the trail of blowdowns and brush. From the summit of Watatic (**Hike #20**), the trail descends northwest past abandoned ski slopes and into the Watatic Wildlife refuge area. The trail enters New Hampshire and continues its 20-mile long bumpy journey past stonewalls deep in the woods, old cellar holes, woods roads, abandoned pastures, and beaver ponds.

The Wapack Trail moves along a skyline route over the open summit ledges of New Ipswich (**Hike #30**) and Barrett Mountain, with a detour to Kidder Mountain (**Hike #2**) and Temple Mountains (**Hikes # 6 & 7**). Boston is visible from some points along the ridge, with side views of farms, fields, and the forested Souhegan, Nashua and Contoocook River Valleys along the way. The Trail ascends Pack Monadnock (**Hike #12**) and terminates on Old Mountain Road beyond the north slope of North Pack Monadnock Mountain (**Hike #11**) in Greenfield. There are numerous entry points on the Wapack Trail as it crosses several roads. A good portion of the footpath passes through privately owned land. Camping is available nearby at the Windblown Ski Touring area on Route 124 in New Ipswich. (Call for reservations, 603-878-2869).

The *Monadnock-Sunapee Greenway* is a 49-mile hiking trail linking Mount Monadnock with Mount Sunapee in Newbury, New Hampshire. Blazed in white rectangles and developed by the *AMC* and *The Society for the Protection of New Hampshire Forests*, the route begins at the summit of Mount Monadnock on the Dublin Trail and continues north, following abandoned roads, pastures, and wilderness trails through small towns, open hardwoods, towering pine, and hemlock forests, state parks, and the Monadnock Highlands (Pitcher Mountain, **Hike #5**) that divide the Connecticut and Merrimack River drainages.

The majority of the corridor crosses privately owned land and it is protected by conservation easements between the Forest Society and over eighty landowners who have worked with the Forest Society's Land Protection Department, as well as through the state-wide Land Conservation Investment Program (LCIP).

All three of these trails lend themselves well for extended hikes and provide excellent opportunities for day hikes because they cross numerous roads and points of access along the way.

View of Mt. Monadnock from Pack Monadnock Mountain

Mount Monadnock

Mount Monadnock is the crown jewel of the region and can be approached from four different towns - Jaffrey, Dublin, Marlborough, and Troy. Mount Monadnock State Park in Jaffrey (603-532-8862) comprises 5,000 acres, with the Park Headquarters located on the southeast hip of the mountain. There is a $2.50 service charge per adult, with camping year round, and *no pets* are allowed. There are six main trails and nearly two dozen connecting trails (totalling 40 miles of trails) that make it easy to climb the mountain without using the same route twice. The most popular sites to begin hikes are on the Old Toll Road (**Hike #16**), and the State Park Headquarters, which offers the most variety of loops. The Marlboro Trail (**Hike #29**) begins off the Shaker Road, 2.1 miles west of the Old Toll Road trailhead.

The most popular trails are also the most direct (White Dot and White Cross, 2 miles each). The White Dot begins near the Warden's office in the state park. The White Cross branches off the White Dot Trail at Falcon Spring (the Spring), then joins the White Dot Trail well above timberline about 1/4 mile below the summit. The Old Toll Road leads 1.3 miles to a large clearing where the Halfway House Hotel burned down in 1954. Several connecting trails lead from the clearing to sub-peaks and the summit. You can have more of a "wilderness experience" by hiking many of the rarely used trails. Excursions should start at the Visitor's Center in the park (open mid-April to Veteran's Day), where you'll find a model of the mountain, displays of history, flora and fauna. Summer hikes are sponsored co-operatively by Monadnock State Park and the Harris Center for Conservation Education. Trail maps are available at the Park Headquarters, along with a skyline panorama map -- a useful tool for identifying towns, lakes, and other mountains from the summit. There is a fixed compass painted on the summit, and a ranger is often stationed on the mountain top to provide interpretative information, Saturday/Sunday from late May to late October.

On a clear day it is possible to identify the Atlantic Ocean and points in all six New England states. The Society for the Protection of New Hampshire Forests (SPNHF) owns the largest portion of the mountain. The area is administered by the State of New Hampshire, Division of Parks and Recreation by lease arrangements. The park was designated a National Natural Landmark in 1982. The Park Headquarters area is located off Route 124 in Jaffrey, providing camping (28 sites), picnic area, visitor's center, toilet facilities, and parking. Plowed parking is provided for winter hiking and cross-country skiing (14 miles of trails). Winter camping is permitted, but the campground road is not plowed. Mount Monadnock hosts over 127,000 visitors every year, making it one of the most climbed mountains in the world.

Map for Hike 1

North Village

SHIELING STATE FOREST

P

Sand Hill Rd.

Old Street Rd.

SANDPIT

N

Contours in feet (20 foot intervals)

USGS: PETERBOROUGH N

0		1/2		1 MILE

0	1000 FEET	0	500 m	1000 m

Printed from TOPO! ©1998 Wildflower Productions (www.topo.com)

1

Shieling Forest

Rating: An easy walking, well-marked loop trail that leads to a glacial erratic, with sidepaths to a wildflower garden and a tree identification trail. An excellent introductory hike for young children.
Distance: 1.5 miles
Hiking time: 1.5 hours
Lowest Elevation: 760 feet
Highest Elevation: 860 feet
USGS Map: Peterborough North
Other Maps: New Hampshire Department of Resources and Economic Development map

The Shieling Forest is a pleasure to hike anytime of the year; each season brings its own subtle beauty. With its behemoth ice age boulders, streamside wildflower garden, and easy walking trails that carry the hiker past a variety of plant and wildlife habitats, it is an ideal place for young families to cut their hiking teeth. Although it is not a state park (Shieling Forest is operated by the New Hampshire Department of Resources and Economic Development), it does have limited picnic facilities and "well-mannered" dogs are welcomed.

A network of over two miles of self-guided trails winds through the 45 acres of forested ridges and valleys which was donated to the state in 1980 by Mrs. Elizabeth Yates McGreal, a long time resident of Peterborough and conservationist, historian and nationally known writer. Mrs.

McGreal also established a trust fund to help defray the maintenance and operation costs of the property which includes her former renovated 1789 dwelling house, office headquarters building, and Forestry Learning Center. A large map in a glassed-in bulletin board outside the Center building details the forest pathways, and a mailbox contains copies of the trail guide/map. The Forestry Learning Center includes an exhibit area and library, and presents a wide variety of programs from pruning to basic orienteering, as well as tree and wildflower identification.

Access: The trailhead can be reached by taking Route 101 West from Milford. Three miles west of the Temple Mountain Ski Area, turn right onto Old Street Road -- use caution because it is a sharp turn downhill. Continue 1.7 miles to a stop sign (Sand Hill Road). Continue straight for another 0.2 miles.

Description: Begin by heading east across a small field in the direction of an unusual sight for a New Hampshire setting: a white mulberry tree. Although the Chinese import looks out of place among its hardwood and evergreen counterparts, it has adapted quite well to its environs and in late July produces a crop of creamy white berries which are a favorite with the birds. After stepping through a gap in a stone wall and descending a set of brick stairs, you'll walk down a steep bank through a red pine forest devoid of a plant understory -- pine is not shade tolerant so it tends to grow dense.

White paint marks on the trees identify the way and sign posts point out the various trails. At the bottom of the hill the trail crosses Dunbar brook on a wooden footbridge. Beyond the brook, the Boulder Trail continues straight ahead (east), but before you continue, take some time to visit the wildflower garden (Brookside Trail) and Hadley Brickyard.

Bunchberry

You can get to both of these points of interest by crossing a second footbridge to the right and south. The Brookside Trail leads to a spectacular wildflower garden maintained by the Peterborough Garden Club. Almost one hundred varieties of wildflowers, shrubs, ferns, trees, mosses, and groundcovers can be viewed here, including trillium, Solomon's seal, hepatica, and wild sarsaparilla, but also the more unusual spice bush and swamp azalea. Be sure to stay on the mulched pathways as this is a delicate area. Markers identify the plants and streamside picnic tables and benches are provided for relaxation.

Brickyard Road leads south to the site of a former Hadley family brickyard at the edge of a large planting of red pine. Brickmaking was once a prominent industry in Peterborough. According to town histories, all but one house built in the town between the years 1800-1870 were fashioned from bricks made locally. (Peterborough used to be known as "Brick City.") If you look closely along the banks of the stream, you can detect pieces of red brick shimmering through the clear water.

Return to the footbridges and continue on the trail to the boulder which rises gradually past a picnic area and stand of white pines nearly 100 feet tall. In colonial times trees such as these were valuable for their use in the making of masts for the British royal navy. At one time, 400-year-old Eastern White Pines grew as high as 200 feet and reached up to ten feet in diameter. A three-striped "broad arrow" mark hewn by an axe was used to reserve the giant trees for the king, and tampering with the conifers resulted in fines and floggings.

Just beyond the pines you'll pass the Flower Trail junction on the left. The Boulder Trail continues through a stand of old sugar maples. Once a productive sugar operation, the Hurricane of 1938 destroyed many of the trees. Shortly the Tree Trail enters to the right (This is a 10-minute walk which identifies several hardwood species by small signs). The white blazed Boulder Trail continues through a magnificent grove of Eastern hemlocks. Hemlocks make excellent screening, serving as a windbreak to provide protection, travel lanes, and food for wildlife. The cones of the hemlock are among the smallest of all tree cones, about 3/4" long, maturing in one year and falling in the spring to provide feed for squirrels who feast on the seeds. Arched by dollops of newly fallen snow or spread like feather dusters, the short, dense needle branches of these trees are a treat to experience anytime of the year.

Just past the hemlocks, the Ridge Trail enters on your right. This ten-minute loop walk carries you through a beautiful open beech forest and large granite outcrop that was once the site of a quarry. Upon close inspection you can see the smooth sides of some of the square pieces of granite and drill holes. In the vicinity of the outcrop is an interesting dead red oak tree displaying a groove lightning scar sliced up its entire side.

Return to the Ridge Trail junction to complete the three-minute walk to the boulder. This stupendous erratic was transported here by the retreating glaciers from the Mount Ascutney area in Vermont 18,000 years ago. Centuries of weathering and frost action have resulted in the splitting of the huge rock. At least 30 feet high and equally as long, young and "young at heart" climbers may wish to spend time exploring the bumps and crevices of these giants before returning.

Sightseeing: If you have time, you may want to visit the Wheeler Trail on town conservation land in Peterborough. The white-blazed trail follows a meandering stream and loops back to a starting point in less than a mile. The parking area and trail sign are located on Route 101, at 0.2 mile downhill from the Route 123 turnoff for Sharon.

Another place to visit is the Casalis Marsh, where birdwatchers can observe waterfowl, flycatchers, wood duck, Virginia Rail, eastern wood duck, pewee, and common yellow throat. Beyond the marsh are ample opportunities for exploration on old roads. Casalis Marsh is located on Route 123 one mile south of the Route 101/123 junction. Look for a sign and parking area on the left side of the road.

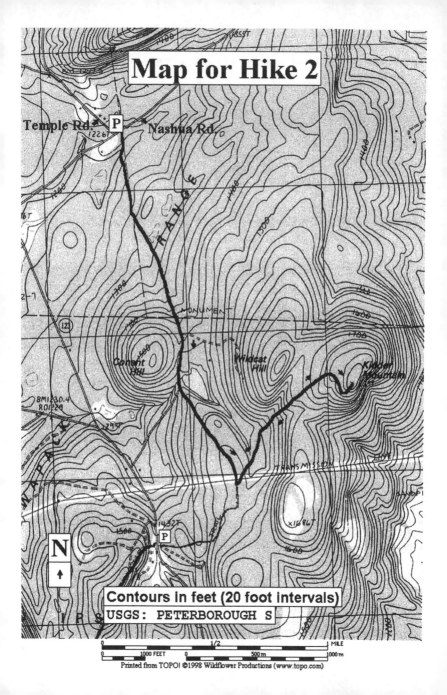

Map for Hike 2

Temple Rd. P Nashua Rd.

Contours in feet (20 foot intervals)
USGS: PETERBOROUGH S

N
↑

Printed from TOPO! ©1998 Wildflower Productions (www.topo.com)

2

Kidder Mountain

Rating: A moderate walk that follows old woods and town dirt roads before continuing through spruce woods to an abandoned blueberry pasture on the summit with wide views of southwestern New Hampshire. There are two possible access points, from the north and the south.
Distance: 5 miles.
Hiking time: 2.5 hours
Lowest elevation: 1,228 feet
Highest elevation: 1,814 feet
USGS Map: Peterborough South
Other Maps: Wapack Trail Guide

This hike to the summit of Kidder Mountain in New Ipswich is slightly off the Wapack Trail, but offers expansive views of southern New Hampshire that makes the detour well worth the effort.

Access: *North Approach.* From the Manchester area, take Route 101 West to Milford. Twelve miles beyond the Milford town oval, turn left onto Route 45 South and continue to Temple. At the southeast corner of the town common, turn right onto the West (Sharon) Road, also known as Nashua Road. 3.2 miles further, at the intersection of Temple Road, the trailhead is marked by a Wapack Trail sign on the left. Park off the shoulder. A small horse barn sits in a field beyond a split-rail fence to the right.

Description: The first leg of the hike follows the Wapack Trail (blazed in yellow triangles) on an old woods road for approximately 1.6 miles. The Wapack Trail sign informs you that the road is closed to vehicles and Route 124 is 2.3 miles distant. One minute after starting out, you'll cross a small stream, then immediately detour onto a path to the right that circumvents the woods road which is muddy and eroded. A small sign here reads HIKERS ONLY. Pine needles and leaves soften your step as you walk past a variety of ground cover that includes partridgeberry, bunchberry, wild lily-of-the-valley, wintergreen, and prince's pine.

Soon the trail crosses the road again, then re-enters the woods to the left. A stone wall is now on your left. The trail rejoins the woods road and moves through a grove of hemlock. About fifteen minutes into the hike, you will reach a trail sign indicating the direction to the Todd Road, to the east. Continue straight ahead and south on the woods road, past a small swamp and cascading brook that parallels the trail on the left. You will ascend at a steady pace through more hemlock and mixed hardwood, then past towering oaks with an understory of striped maple, which you can distinguish by its double toothed leaf margin and green and white vertical stripes in the bark of young trunks. Striped maple is sometimes called Goosefoot Maple because the three shallow lobes at the apex of the wide leaves resemble a webbed foot.

Just beyond the oaks you will come to a dirt town road. A driveway on the left leads to a private residence. Continuing on, you reach a pond with the sign "Wildcat Partnership: No Trespassing." Beyond the pond, the trail continues southeast into the woods on a wide, grassy path. In fifteen minutes you will come to an area cleared for powerlines overhead. At this point you leave the Wapack Trail (which continues south for 0.6 miles to Routes 123/124), and follow the sign onto the blue-blazed Kidder Mountain Trail.

The Kidder Mountain Trail is almost one mile long and starts east on a rocky path that follows the power line. Meadow-sweet, steeplebush, goldenrod, sheep laurel, and wood aster grow along the trail, as do raspberry and blueberry bushes.

Shortly you will cross a small stream beside which grow mountain holly shrubs. More commonly found in northern latitudes, this tall, colorful shrub will capture your attention with its elliptical-shaped leaves and dull red velvet berries. This tall wetlands plant has good wildlife value because its berries survive through the winter after the leaves fall off.

After passing beneath the power line, the trail continues into the woods. Five minutes walk brings you to an area that was clear-cut in 1998; five minutes more and you're back into a spruce woods, with ledges, juniper and blueberry bushes. The trail continues through another clear-cut (be careful to note trail markers here) before reaching the summit, which is marked by a blue triangle on a big boulder. Stone walls and exposed bedrock ledge indicate that you are standing on what was once a pasture. Scrub oak, gray birch, and red spruce poke up through a blanket of blueberry bushes which ripen in August. Kidder Mountain itself descends somewhat, then expands into a tableland known as Flat Mountain. There is an expansive view to the south and southeast of ponds, farms, gleaming metal roofs, and open fields among wooded hills. To the southwest, multi-summited Barrett Mountain stretches in a continuous ridge on its way to Mount Watatic just over the border to Ashburnham, Massachusetts, 3.5 miles away.

Access: *South Approach.* At the trailhead for the north approach (Temple Road junction), continue on Nashua Road for 0.6 miles to Route 123. Turn left onto Route 123 South. After 0.1 mile you will reach the 123/124 junction. Continue south on 123/124 for 0.6 miles to the site of the old Wapack Lodge, which was struck by lightning and burned in the summer of 1993. Look for a sign that says "Wapack Road" (dead end), a private drive. Park on the road shoulder or at a parking area off Old Rindge Road opposite the lodge site. Look for a Wapack Trail sign, indicating distances to Nashua Road, Temple Mountain Ledges, and Route 101.

The trail starts out on a dirt road but immediately enters the woods on the left. Several minutes later you will descend into a clearing with a residence on the right (beware of dog), and continue up a hill to re-enter the woods. After five minutes, the trail turns left and north. Soon you will emerge at the power lines and Kidder Mountain trailhead. From Route 123/124 this is 0.6 mile, about 15 minutes walk.

SEAL OF THE STATE OF NEW HAMPSHIRE
1776

TEMPLE GLASS FACTORY

Was located at a secluded site in the southwest portion of Temple township. Founded in 1780 by Robert Hewes who employed Hessian mercenaries from the British Army trained in the art of glass-blowing. This early attempt to manufacture bottles and crude window-glass was beginning of glass-making in New Hampshire.

Sightseeing: If you have time, you may want to drive to New Ipswich to explore the Barrett House, located at 79 Main Street (Route 123A), a stately mansion built in 1800 by Charles Barrett, Sr., as a wedding gift for his son. Barrett was instrumental in promoting the textile industry in New Ipswich, the site of the first cotton factory in New Hampshire, built in 1803.

The Barrett House is a fine example of Federalist architecture. Operated by the Society for the Preservation of New England Antiquities, the House is open Saturday and Sunday June 1 to October 15, with guided tours every hour from 11 a.m. to 4 p.m. (603-878-2517)

The nearby town of Temple is full of history and also worth investigating. Temple is the site of the first glass works in New Hampshire; it was established in 1780 by Robert Hewes, a soap and tallow chandler from Boston. At this time, the British had blockaded northern ports and prevented window glass and bottles from entering the colonies. Because the colonists were prevented by the British from manufacturing glassware for themselves, Hewes chose a remote location. He established his glass factory on the north slope of Kidder Mountain, and is credited with producing bulls-eye glass, a brilliantly-hued, high quality optical glass with a thickened center ("bulls-eye") left by the glassworker's rod.

Temple is one of the few towns in New Hampshire where the cultural, religious, and civic activities are still centered in buildings standing on the common. Nearby are the village cemetery and a row of classic white New England structures-- an old store, post office, Congregational Church, Town Hall, and the 1842 Miller Grange, formerly the Universalist Church. At the end of the row is the Solon Mansfield Memorial Library (built in 1890).

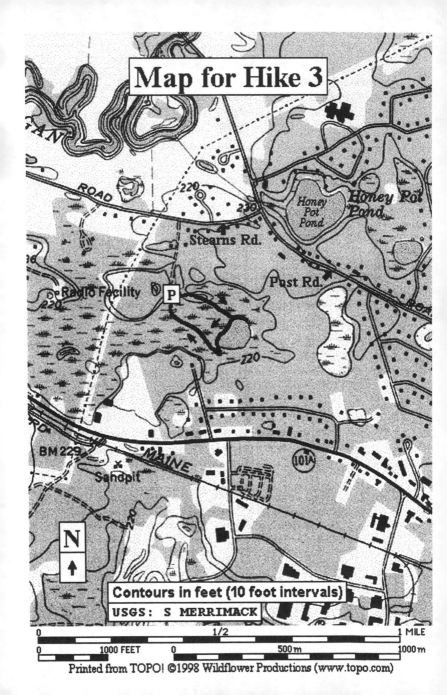

3

Ponemah Bog

Rating: An easy boardwalk stroll over the quaking mat of a kettle hole bog that is home to leatherleaf, cotton grass, pitcher plants, sundews, and other curious insect-eating plants.
Distance: 3/4 mile
Hiking time: 1/2 hour
Pond Elevation: 210 feet
USGS Map: South Merrimack
Other Maps: Audubon Society of New Hampshire map

Like all kettle-hole bogs, the Penomah Bog will one day complete the natural pond succession to become dry land. The encircling mat of sphagnum moss will inexorably squeeze in on the three acres of open water where partial decay and burial will convert it to peat. In time, trees and shrubs will gain a foothold on the organic foundation to wipe away all evidence that a glacial lake ever existed here. But the good news is that you've got more than a few centuries to visit before this all takes place.

Ponemah Bog is a legacy of the ice age. About 13,000 years ago, when the last glaciers retreated north, huge blocks of ice were left, embedded in the ground. As the climate warmed and the frozen chunks melted, the earth caved in to form steeply sloped depressions we know as kettle hole ponds. At Ponemah you'll find examples of the special vegetation able to adapt to this nutrient-lacking habitat: the curious pitcher plants, sundew, and bladderwort (all of which feast on insects), bog laurel, sphagnum moss, rhodora, tufted bog cotton, leather-leaf, and waterwillow.

Ponemah Bog is operated by the Audubon Society of New Hampshire and is open year round from dawn to dusk, with no charge to visit the bog. The entire 3/4-mile trail (including the pond loop) takes only half an hour to complete, but you'll want to spend extra time exploring the wealth of curious plants and savoring the solitude of the otherworld of the bog.

Ponemah is a special place to visit in late spring when the vegetation is in full bloom. While one area may bloom earlier than another, you'll see a bold riot of pinks, yellows, lavenders, and bright whites. In the fall, blueberry bushes and red maples provide vibrant color. The bog is also special in winter when russet-colored blankets of leatherleaf sprawl across the marsh and the moss has frozen into delicate white filigrees like icing on a wedding cake. In winter, you can look for interesting patterns of plants frozen beneath the surface like flowers encased in glass paperweights. You'll see sphagnum spreading like a spongy pale green blanket, but in other places massed in yellow and maroon mounds along the shoreline. Melting crystals of ice glitter like jewels between the dense hummocks of grass. Listen to the delicate crinkling of ice melting as the sun climbs higher in the afternoon sky. As you approach the pond loop, tamarack, and black spruce stand naked in black silhouettes against the sky and the pond surface glistens in the late afternoon like a fire. The bog appears lifeless but there are frogs, insects, and turtles resting beneath the frozen surface or hidden in crevices.

Access: Ponemah Bog is located in Amherst, New Hampshire. To get there, take exit 8 on the Everett Turnpike in Nashua. Follow Route 101-A West for three miles to South Merrimack. Turn right onto the Boston Post Road and continue for two miles. Turn left on Stearns Road. After 0.2 mile turn left again onto Rhodora Road which turns to dirt after a short distance. Park near a trailhead sign.

Description: The yellow-blazed trail begins at the parking area on the high ground of an upland forest. The familiar birch, maple, and oak grow here but so too does pitch pine -- a three needled conifer with deeply furrowed bark more common to the sandier southern soils. Pitch pine produces closed cones that remain on the trees for years.

Be sure to keep an eye out for chickadees, jays, titmice, a wide variety of sparrows, thrushes, and other birds. You're likely to hear the persistent tapping of a woodpecker or you may spy a raptor searching the landscape for unsuspecting rodents. At first you may feel like you're on a neighborhood stroll as voices from children playing in the back yards of residences drift toward you from the edge of the woods. The aroma of sweet fern scents the air, and in the spring, ferns curled up like fiddleheads and the membranous pink globes of lady slipper poke up from the wet ground at the edge of the trail. Ponemah Bog has quite a collection of native orchids, including whorled pogonia, ladyslippers and liparis. There are 35 native species of wild orchids in New Hampshire.

Shortly, the trail branches to the right to lead to an observation platform. This perch allows a good view of the subtle colors of the low brush and tawny grasses stretching to the open water in the distance. Looking out at this sparse expanse of stunted trees and shrubs, it is hard to imagine that this was once a 100-acre lake. Return to the main trail. Soon you'll walk by a marsh bursting with clouds of pink Rhodora in May. Rhodora is especially showy as its flowers appear before its leaves unfold.

You'll step onto a boardwalk as you approach the vast expanse of the bog mat. Here you'll find wiry-stemmed leatherleaf, also called cassandra, a low shrub with tough leathery leaves and white bell-like flowers hanging in lines of a dozen or more underneath its stem in the spring. In June, you'll see bog laurel which displays a pink cup-like flower. As you continue on the boardwalk, swampcandle and white tufts of bog cotton show themselves among the floating web of sedge and moss which is thick enough so that shrubs and birch, pitch pine, and other trees are able to take root.

Minutes later, the open water of the bog appears in the distance. You may want to reach over and squeeze a spongy mass of pale green sphagnum moss. Some species of this moss can absorb well over ten times its own weight in water. Sphagnum was dried and used as a diaper material by the Indians and as a surgical dressing during World War I. Sometime in the 1940s, the bog was used to harvest peat moss, which develops from sphagnum. Peat was cut with a shovel and hauled to a drying shed, where it was ground and then shipped to greenhouses. Peat was also used as a fuel.

Turn left at a junction as you approach the pond. You'll notice a distinct spring in the wooden planks as the thickness of the mat tapers toward the edge of the pond. Follow the boardwalk to an observation platform. Look for grass pink, a showy pink-flowered member of the orchid family, and the unusual insect-eating plants which are much smaller than their Little Shop of Horror reputations. The show stealer has to be the remarkable pitcher plant. The delicate paper-thin green and red veined leaves of this vessel-like plant secrete a fragrant syrup that insects can't resist. Once an insect is caught, the slippery hairs around the lip of the leaves, like the withes of a lobster trap, hasten the victim's trip downward. Digestive juices do the rest.

You'll have to bend down to see the red sundew plant, which resembles a tiny burdock. Lured by the "dew" on its round leaves, the insect is wrapped by small hairs and then digested by the plant enzymes. Another insectivorous plant grows here, the slender yellow bladderwort with flowers resembling the snap-dragon like flowers.

Ferns, leatherleaf, bog laurel, and bog rosemary present a visual treat of contrasting summer greens. Yellow pond lilies bob on the rippling surface of the water. Also thriving in these boggy conditions are the feathery tamarack, red maple, and black spruce, a small tree with dark cones and thin grayish scaly bark. The cones of the black spruce may remain on the tree for decades. The only conifer to shed its needles each fall, tamarack (American larch) does not reach great heights growing through the wet moss of the bog. Its long tough roots were used by the Indians to sew together their birch-bark canoes. Return to the junction and continue on the boardwalk to the other viewing platforms. Toward the end of the pond loop, the boardwalk continues through a brushy section before taller conifers signal you are approaching higher ground and the end of the trail. Minutes later you'll find yourself back at the parking area.

Sightseeing: In nearby Milford, the 285-acre Tucker Brook Town Forest provides opportunities to explore wetlands, pine groves, glacial erratics, beaver ponds, a waterfall, and mill dam sites. The two entrances into the Tucker Brook Town Forest are located off Boulder Drive and Savage Road. You can also visit an old granite quarry operation on the Mayflower Hill Town Forest trail which has an access in two areas, on Shady Lane and at the end of Falconer Avenue Extension.

The highlight of the Hitchiner Town Forest is 751-foot Burns Hill with open, sunny granite outcroppings, blueberry bushes and views to the west. The Hitchiner Town Forest is located off Mullen Road. The Milford Conservation Commission maintains two shorter trails that follow the Souhegan River. The Souhegan River Trail begins at the Milford Fish Hatchery land on North River Road. The Emerson Park Trail begins near the Milford Post Office. Free maps are available at Milford Town Hall.

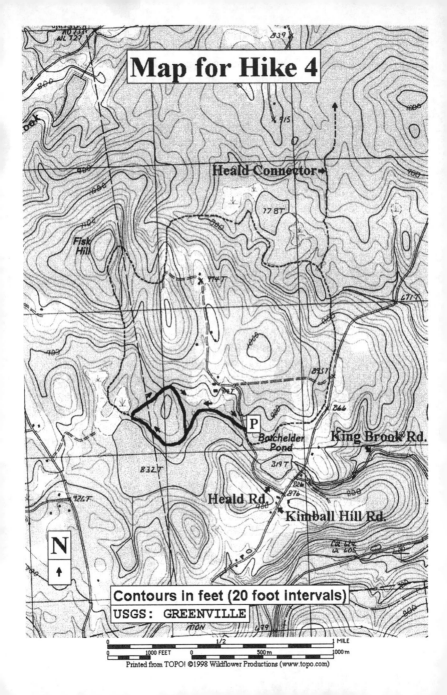

Map for Hike 4

Heald Connector →

Fisk
Hill

P

Batchelder
Pond

King Brook Rd.

Heald Rd.

Kimball Hill Rd.

N
↑

Contours in feet (20 foot intervals)

USGS: GREENVILLE

0   1/2   1 MILE
0   1000 FEET 0   500m   1000 m

Printed from TOPO! ©1998 Wildflower Productions (www.topo.com)

4

The Heald Tract

Rating: An easy forested walk past a variety of wildlife habitats along the edge of a flood control pond.
Distance: 2 miles, with optional extension to 5 miles
Hiking time: 1 hour, with optional extension to 3 hours
Pond elevation: 835 feet
USGS Map: Greenville
Other Maps: Heald Tract map

Featured on this summitless hike are meadows, wetlands, old cellar holes, ponds, orchards, wildlife habitats, an abandoned farmstead, blue heron rookery, and magnificent open beech woods. Located on the Wilton-Temple town line, the Heald Tract is a preserve of the Society for the Protection of New Hampshire Forests (SPNHF). Donated in 1986 by the Heald Trust, the property has grown to more than 500 acres and encompasses over six miles of foot paths and interpretive trails for passive recreation and nature learning opportunities.

25 information stations, marked by blue and yellow signs, identify natural features along the way. The centerpiece of the Heald Tract is a 69-acre wildlife pond, the result of a flood control and watershed protection project completed in 1964. The pond here is the haunt of many species of waterfowl during the seasonal migration periods. Waterproof footwear is advisable as the trail is sometimes wet. Canoeing and boating are not allowed, but foot trails lead to fishing areas. The Heald Tract is open year round. Maps are available from Phil Heald, Jr., 168 Heald Road, Wilton NH 03086. A trail guide containing activities for kids is available free to teachers and youth leaders (Call SPNHF in Concord, 224-9945).

Access: To reach the trailhead, take Route 101 West to Route 31 South in Wilton. Continue on 31 South toward Greenville for 2.5 miles. Turn right onto King Brook Road, a pleasant uphill drive of 0.9 mile that winds alongside a tumbling brook bordered by feathery hemlocks. At the road's end, turn left onto Kimball Hill Road. Continue uphill for 0.1 mile, and turn right at a big red barn onto Heald Road. Drive 0.3 mile, past a Heald Tract Forest Society sign and park at the second pull-off on the right.

Note: This area is rich in mountain laurel, an evergreen shrub with spectacular white and purple clustered flowers which blooms from early June to early July. Good viewing areas include Route 31 from Wilton to Greenville and south to the Massachusetts border, as well as Route 123 through Mason and Route 101 from Milford to Peterborough.

Description: The two-mile-long Pond Trail, blazed in yellow, begins opposite the parking area. After moving through a stand of white pine with an impressive understory of mountain laurel, the trail follows the north shore of the pond for nearly a mile. Sedges, reeds, and the spikes of cattail grow here in the shallow water. You will also see partridgeberry, leatherleaf, arrowwood, Canada lily, and polypody ferns before the trail widens as it moves through a grove of hemlock. In August, the New York ironweed displays its brilliant hairlike clusters of lavender flowers on the bank near the dam site and flood control monument. Ironweed gets its name from the rigidity of the stem.

Near Station #11, a long, sloping stone wall rambles along a hillside. It is believed that these fences were originally built to mark boundaries of once open fields and pasture, now overgrown by woods. Just beyond a huge, gnarled white pine, the trail moves through an open field, then swings down to the pond. Near an abandoned beaver lodge, purple pickerel weed and jewelweed brighten the water's edge. Jewelweed has particular value for hikers because its tiny pendant-like orange flowers can be rubbed on the skin as an emergency antidote to poison ivy. Coincidentally, jewelwood often grows near poison ivy.

Just ahead, the trail emerges at a clearing. To the right, two old barns sit deteriorating on the slope of a hillside orchard. In late May, viola and wild strawberry grow in the marshy area near the pond here. In late summer, you'll find the soft, bristled, purple flowers of the Joe Pye weed, which are especially attractive to butterflies. According to folklore, Joe Pye was an Indian medicine man who lived in colonial Massachusetts and used the plant to cure typhus fever.

The trail re-enters the woods near Station #16 and moves past a shoreline boulder outlook where you can sit and contemplate the rippling waters, the delicate yellow blossoms of water lilies, and the twittering chorus of insects and birds. Continuing on the trail, you will approach a double marker and Heald Junction sign. The Ledge Trail, which will be your return route, heads north. Continue straight ahead and west over the gentle woodland terrain.

At Station #21, there is club moss blanketing the forest floor with its tiny brown cone-like spore cases and erect, branching stems. Club moss is also known by other names, such as crow foot, creeping Jenny, standing spruce, and ground pine. There are about 50 types of club mosses in the United States. Although it is hard to imagine from its 6-inch height, the ancestors of this low evergreen plant once attained heights of 100 feet in primeval swamps. Today, coal is produced from the remains of such swamps, and many states have laws protecting this important ground cover. The club moss has a creeping stem running beneath dead leaves that prevents soil from being washed away. Shortly you'll come to the Pond Trail/Ledge junction. (The Ledge Trail is your return route.)

At Station #22, a sign indicates *The Trail to the Point*. Be sure to take this detour; it is a short walk to an overlook at the edge of the pond, a perfect spot to enjoy lunch and the solitude of the surroundings. There's a good chance you'll see a wood duck or blue heron, or hear the hammering of a piliated woodpecker as it seeks insect larvae in the bark of dying trees. After you've rested, return to the yellow trail to follow the shoreline with its broken stumps and grasses.

After moving past a high, abandoned beaver lodge at Station #25, you will come to a junction with the blue-blazed Fisk Hill Trail. Continue on the yellow trail, moving uphill to the right and east. After 300 yards, you will reach the Ledge Cut off on the right. This 10-minute walk takes you past hemlock, an airy grove of beech trees, and scalloped ledges, and brings you back to the Pond Trail Junction. Turn left to retrace your steps to the parking area.

Optional Extension: If you have time, take the 3-mile Fisk Hill and Camp Trail, blazed in blue. This will lead you on an adventure over the slopes of Fisk Hill, then to an orchard with a great view of the Lyndeborough Mountains, Joe English Hill, the Uncanoonucs, and Crotched Mountain to the north. The trail continues northerly and goes down into the woods past a beaver pond with a blue heron rookery, where nests sit atop dead trees. The trail moves onto a camp lot and 3-acre pond held back by a cut-stone dam, past a series of cellar holes off an old road, magnificent open beech woods, an orchard, and briefly along the shoreline of Batchelder Pond, before ending at Heald Road near the parking area.

Another *option* is the Pratt Pond Trail, which features old railway tunnels and waterfalls and was opened to the public in 1995. This 5-mile route begins off the Kimball Hill Road (0.5 mile from the junction with Heald Road) near an old cellar hole, moves on to the bridge at Route 31, crosses the Souhegan River, and continues to Pratt Pond in Mason.

Sightseeing: You may want to visit Sheldrick Forest, a recently acquired 227-acre Nature Conservancy preserve of old pine, red oak, and hemlock, where large sections have been undisturbed for more than 150 years. The great size, age, and species diversity of this forest make it one of the best examples of transitional hardwood-conifer, and a habitat for migratory songbirds and other wide-ranging animals. To get there from the Heald Tract, return to Route 101, drive west for two miles, and turn left onto Temple (West End) Road just beyond Gary's Harvest Restaurant. After 0.4 mile, turn left onto Town Farm Road. Continue uphill (the road turns to dirt surface) for 0.7 mile. The Sheldrick Forest is joined to the Heald Tract by the 0.9-mile Heald Connector. The connecting trail starts off the Swift Way and joins the Heald Tract system at the Castor Pond Trail just north of "The Rocks."

On the way to Sheldrick Forest, you may want to visit an interesting memorial marking the spot where Captain Sam Greele was killed by the fall of a tree on September 25, 1798. While riding on horseback to attend a public hearing in Wilton Center, Greele was struck by a tree blown over by a high wind. Today, a simple marble obelisk on a square base marks the tragic spot.

To get to the monument, take Route 101 west from intersection with Route 31. Turn left onto Russell Hill Road 0.9 mile from the Route 31 intersection. The monument, surrounded by a rusted iron fence, is located 0.6 mile further down Russell Hill Road under a grove of hemlock trees on the left side.

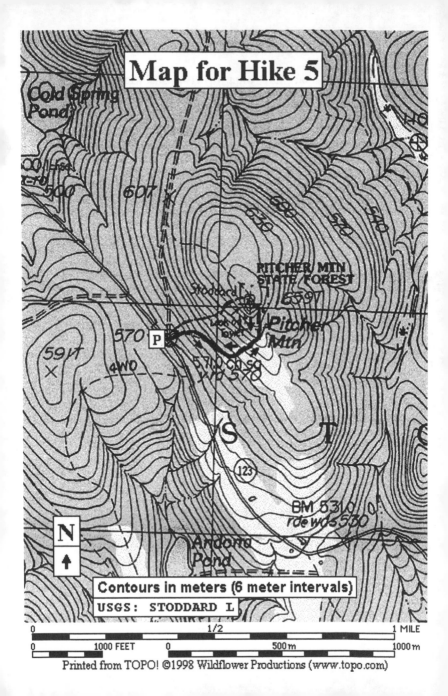

Map for Hike 5

Cold Spring Pond

607

630

600 570 540

PITCHER MTN
STATE FOREST

659

Stoddard T.

570 **P** Pitcher Mtn

591
X

4WD

570 On 570
470 570

S   T

123

BM 531
rd e wds 530

N
↑

Andorra
Pond

Contours in meters (6 meter intervals)

USGS: STODDARD L

| 0 | 1/2 | 1 MILE |

| 0 | 1000 FEET | 0 | 500 m | 1000 m |

Printed from TOPO! ©1998 Wildflower Productions (www.topo.com)

5

Pitcher Mountain

Rating: An easy hike on a section of the Monadnock-Sunapee Greenway that leads to an overgrown pasture on the summit, and an outstanding 360-degree view of the Monadnock Highlands.
Distance: 0.8 mile
Hiking time: 1/2 hour
Lowest Elevation: 2,000 feet
Highest Elevation: 2,153 feet
USGS Map: Stoddard
Other Maps: Monadnock-Sunapee Greenway Trail Guide

Pitcher Mountain today is part of the Andorra Forest, a lush 11,000-acre SPNHF preserve, the largest one in New Hampshire protected by private easement, and prime habitat for the wildlife of the region. Standing on the steps of the Pitcher Mountain observation tower and gazing out at the gently rolling hills, it is difficult to realize that this area was once a charred wasteland. But in April, 1941, the Great Marlow-Stoddard forest fire turned 27,000 acres of this bucolic scene into a smoldering ruin. The fire first broke out near a logging operation, then zigzagged out of control, forcing the wildlife to scatter before the onrush of smoke and flames. The spring of 1941 had been unusually dry -- April was the driest in seventy years; and the Hurricane of 1938 had provided many downed and damaged trees for kindling. The Great Fire is recorded as one of the most destructive in the history of southern New Hampshire.

This hike to Pitcher Mountain is within everyone's ability. It begins on the Greenway, a 49-mile-long footpath that connects Mount Monadnock in Jaffrey and Mount Sunapee in Newbury. The Monadnock-Sunapee Greenway Trail Guide is available from the Society for the Preservation of New Hampshire Forests, 54 Portsmouth St., Concord NH 03301.

Access: From the Manchester area, take Route 101 West to Peterborough. Continue north on Route 123 to Hancock. Continue 10 miles to Stoddard. One mile west of Stoddard is the Pitcher Mountain Farm (open daily to the public 6 a.m. to 4 p.m.). The parking area and trailhead to Pitcher Mountain is 1/2 mile north of the Farm.

Description: Two roads branch off from the parking area. Start your hike on the one that leads east (to the right), which is blazed in white rectangles. The road to the left is the Hubbard Hill Road which will cross the Greenway at 2/3 mile ahead. After crossing Route 123 at the parking lot, the Greenway travels the fire warden's road 0.4 mile up the south side of Pitcher. Along the way you'll get a nice view of Mount Monadnock across a pasture before reaching the fire warden's cabin just below the Pitcher Mountain fire tower. An alternate route is a shorter but steeper and rockier blue-blazed trail which enters the woods immediately after you start out on the Greenway. Either trail, white or blue, takes only 15 minutes to complete.

The 50-foot fire tower is manned from April to October, and hikers are welcome to visit the observation cab if the watchman isn't busy spotting fires. Because there are no trees in the immediate vicinity, the view from the top is a spectacular 360-degrees. You can see Mount Monadnock to the south, Lovewell to the north, Kearsarge to the northeast, and Crotched Mountain and the Wapack Range to the southeast.

Sunapee stands slightly beyond Lovewell to the west, the big mountain to the northwest is Mount Ascutney in Vermont. Killington is a four-peaked mountain to the left of Ascutney. As you look toward Killington and direct your gaze southwest along the line of mountain tops, you can see all the well-known ski areas of Vermont: Okemo, Magic, and Bromley. South of Bromley you can see Stratton, Snow, Haystack, and on a clear day, Hogback. To the east, Hyland Lake nestles serenely in a forested pocket.

All of the distant blue hills of the region comprise the rocky divide between the Merrimack and Connecticut Rivers known as the Monadnock Highlands. Town histories report that rain falling on one side of a house located in Stoddard trickles into the Merrimack River, while rain from the other side makes its way into the Connecticut River.

After enjoying the view, you may want to follow the white-blazed Greenway further before returning to your car. The Greenway continues north along the ridge of Pitcher. Be particularly careful here because there is a maze of sidepaths, courtesy of the blueberry pickers.

View from Pitcher Mountain

6

Temple Mountain (North)

Rating: A moderate walk up a ski trail that leads to out-croppings of granite, offering panoramic views of the Souhegan and Contoocook River Valleys.
Distance: 2.8 miles
Hiking time: 2 hours
Lowest Elevation: 1,485 feet
Highest Elevation: 1,987 feet
USGS Map: Peterborough South
Other Maps: Wapack Trail Guide and Map

While most people recognize Temple Mountain as a popular New Hampshire ski area, it can be an outdoors attraction in summer as well. A section of the 21-mile-long Wapack Trail stretches over its summit, making this an ideal hiking destination within an hour's drive of the population centers of southern New Hampshire. A long, north-to-south axis of monadnocks, resembling a serpent's back and following the path of the ancient glaciers, the Temple Mountain ridgeline is comprised of five separate summits. And while the north summit sees plenty of skiing action from December to March, many of the other peaks offer summer solitude and breathtaking panoramic views for those willing to lace up a pair of boots. Of these vantage points, the one that offers the best views is known as Temple Mountain Ledges, a 1,987-foot outcropping of granite straddling the Temple-Sharon town line which can easily be reached in an hour's walking time.

Temple Mountain Ski Area lift

Access: To get to the Temple Mountain Ledges trailhead from the Manchester area, follow Route 101 West to the Temple Mountain Ski Area in Peterborough Gap, 15 miles west of Milford. Park your car in the Temple Mountain Ski Area front lot. Please note this is private property.

Note: Parking is also available in the Miller State Park base lot (0.1 mile west of Temple Mountain Ski area on Route 101). You may be charged a $2.50 fee, especially during the busy fall season. New Hampshire residents under 12 and over 65 are free. A trailhead sign is on the south side of the highway across from the Miller State Park lot. Use caution approaching the trailhead. This is a busy stretch of highway.

Description: The 1.4-mile trail, which is blazed with yellow triangles (Wapack Trail) painted on trees and rocks, follows a southeasterly direction, and begins opposite the entranceway to Miller State Park. The trailhead sign directs you into the woods, but within seconds you'll emerge at two large unpaved parking areas. Look for a *No Campfires* sign and yellow blaze in the second (upper) lot.

You'll walk through low brush, passing wooden equipment sheds to your left as the trail continues uphill. In a few minutes a dirt road directs you to a wide, grassy ski trail to the right (Broadway), which in late summer is spiked with a wildflower cornucopia of wood aster, meadowsweet, clover, golden rod, and bottled gentians. As you walk uphill, turn around for a good view of Pack Monadnock Mountain and the blue hills of south central New Hampshire rising beyond. The whisper of automobiles traveling Route 101 below can be heard, but you'll feel miles removed from civilization.

You'll leave the dirt road which turns to the left. Continue walking up the ski trail. At the top of the ski trail, watch for the yellow blazes. To the left of a small wooden shed-like building, the hiking trail continues down a grassy path and follows a dirt road along a fringe of woods. A few minutes later, near a gray equipment shed, the trail turns right into a spruce and birch woods. The trail snakes its way upward over slabs of ledge for several minutes before once again emerging at a ski trail. Continue walking uphill, paralleling the lift line station and a communications tower surrounded by a chain link fence. This signals the end of the steepest portion of the hike, and you may want to take a short break to walk over to view the long line of blue chairs strangely silent as they stretch to the base area below against the backdrop of Pack Monadnock Mountain.

When you are ready to go on, look for a red-and-white ski touring sign at the entrance to the woods. From here the trail is an easy jaunt over a needle-padded path that carries you past stone walls, waving ferns, and cairns. In ten minutes you'll come to a tall singular cairn marking a ledge area. It may appear as though you have arrived at your destination because the view suddenly opens up. But continue walking on the trail five minutes more past several smaller cairns.

You'll know for certain that you have arrived at the Temple Mountain Ledges when you see seven monument-like cairns. With the sudden surprise of these unusual figures looming on the expansive ledges above you, you may feel as though you've stumbled upon a sacrificial altar of the ancients. The views from the top are no less magical. Directly to the south looms the wooded dome of Holt Peak and Burton Peak beyond. Holt Peak (2,084 feet) is the main summit of the Temple Mountain ridgeline. The undulating green country-side of the Souhegan Valley unfolds to the southeast, while the Uncanoonuc Mountains and whalebacked Joe English Hill capture your eyes to the northeast. Grand Monadnock is on the horizon to the west. The breezy ledges are an inviting place to have lunch or test a pair of binoculars on fluffy cloud formations drifting by overhead. If you have the urge to explore, a three-minute walk south on the trail will bring you to another cairn-topped ledge area with good views west.

The Wapack Trail -- the oldest interstate hiking trail in the Northeast

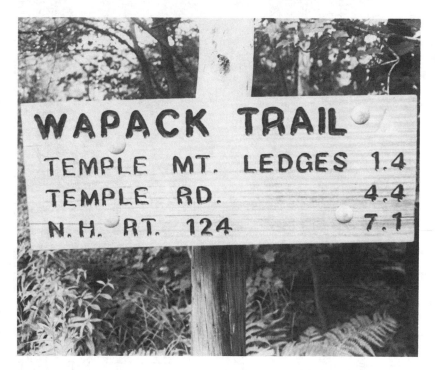

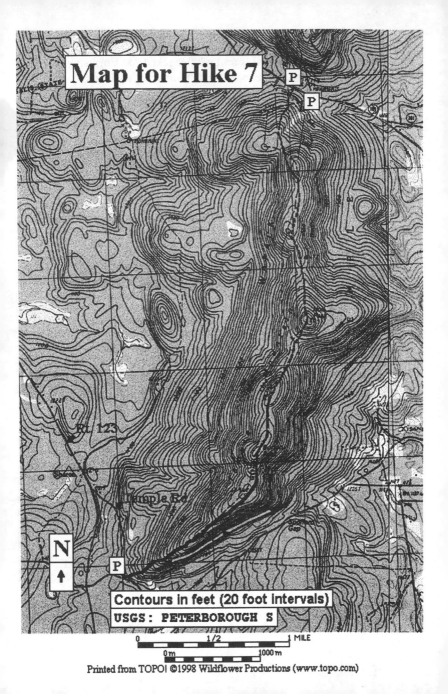

Map for Hike 7

P

P

Rt. 123

Temple Rd

N

P

Contours in feet (20 foot intervals)

USGS: PETERBOROUGH S

0   1/2   1 MILE

0 m   1000 m

Printed from TOPO! ©1998 Wildflower Productions (www.topo.com)

7

Temple Mountain (South)

Rating: An out-and-back hike that follows the Wapack Trail past stone walls, abandoned pastures, and sunny ledges that offer good views of the Souhegan River Valley along the way to Burton Peak. An optional longer walk carries you over the ridge line of the Temple Mountain system.
Distance: 2.8 miles (optional extension 4.3 miles)
Hiking time: 3 hours (optional extension 4 hours)
Lowest elevation: 1,297 feet
Highest elevation: 2,020-foot Burton Peak (optional extension is the 2,084-foot Holt Peak)
USGS Map: Peterborough South
Other Maps: Wapack Trail Guide map

To hike the south end of Temple Mountain is like taking a walk on the wild side. There are panoramic views of the Souhegan Valley from several bare outlooks along the less civilized south end of the system as it gradually curves northeastward toward Holt Peak, which is Temple Mountain's 2,084-foot main summit. If you are up to the challenge of exploring long forgotten stone walls, abandoned pastures, and clusters of bluebead lilies and other woodland plants, you can hike the nearly five-mile long ridge line. This will require a friend and two cars, leaving one vehicle in the Miller State Park base parking lot off Route 101 in Peterborough Gap; the other car at the south foot of Temple Mountain, and hiking between your parked cars. If a half-day outing is more your style, then there are plenty of good outlooks that provide a real sense of serenity only one-half mile into this lightly hiked section of the Wapack Trail.

Access: The trailhead can be reached by taking Route 101 West from Milford. Three miles west of the Temple Mountain Ski Area, turn left onto Route 123. Drive four miles south and turn left again (just beyond the Sharon Arts Center) onto Temple Road, which goes uphill and narrows. After 0.7 mile look for a small parking area on the right.

Optional Extension: Leave one car in the base lot of the Temple Mountain Ski Area or the Miller State Park base lot. During the busy fall season you may be charged $2.50 per person to park in the Miller State Park lot (NH residents 12 and under or over 65 are free). Leave a second car in the parking area at the south foot of Temple Mountain. Hike from car to car.

Description: The trail starts off steeply on a wide, rocky path that climbs past maple, hemlock, birch, and several gigantic red pines. Immediately to the left is a Wapack Trail mapboard and a sign indicating that the next 2.2 miles of trail are the Cabot Skyline. You'll continue past an abandoned two-story cabin, its shingles blackened by years of weathering. At this point you'll continue uphill into the privately-owned Avelinda Forest. Small metal signs fastened to trees urge you to use caution here so that others may enjoy the beauty of this area. Notice the long stone wall running uphill. Along the way you'll see it again and again, carefully constructed of flat rocks forming part of the border between the towns of Temple and Sharon. Indeed, on some old maps, the Temple Mountains are referred to as the Boundary Mountains.

After 10 minutes you will see an opening near the wall on the right, which offers a good view south toward Barrett Mountain. From here the trail continues gradually uphill in a northeast direction over a sunny ledge. To the northeast is an eye-stretching view of Mount Monadnock, Gap, and Little Monadnock mountains, giving way to the rolling countryside as it ambles toward Massachusetts.

Along the trail to Holt Peak

Continuing on the trail two minutes more brings you to a cairn and sign that marks an outlook. If you take a few steps to your right off the path, there is a fine view to the south. You'll spy 1,832-foot Mount Watatic in Ashburnham, Massachusetts, 11 miles away. Behind it sits 2,006-foot Mount Wachusett just south of Fitchburg, Massachusetts. Both of these mountains are scarred with ski trails, and binoculars will show that Mount Wachusett is crowned with an observation tower.

As you continue, young maple, birch, oak, and low bush blueberry fill in the ledgy trailside, along with a few spruce trees. In a few minutes you'll enter a stretch of woods dominated by slender white birch trees where a noticeable drop in temperature will be a welcome relief. After a few minutes more of walking past two grotesquely misshapen beech trees, the bark of which someone has initialed, you'll come to a sun-warmed boulder to the left which provides an excellent rest spot and another great view. In the foreground, slightly southeast to south, lie Kidder Mountain, Wildcat and Conant Hills. Watatic Mountain anchors the view in the distance while the long multi-summited ridge of Barrett Mountain in New Ipswich stretches off to the southwest. There's a good chance you will see a hawk soaring the thermals.

From the boulder outlook, a 10-minute walk past several more cairns takes you back into the woods, but this time the path will be needle-covered and evergreen-shaded, reminding you of the conifers up north. From this point the view will be limited, but this stretch is rewarding nevertheless. There is a real sense of isolation here, the still quiet broken only by the squeaky tick of a bird, the high pitched kissing sound of chipmunks, or the scurrying of a small animal in the woods.

A highlight of this woodland walk is the clusters of bluebead-lily plants (also called Clintonia; named after DeWitt Clinton, governor of New York, 1769-1818. The fruits of this plant are extraordinarily true-blue). Shortly you will see a small sign informing you that you've reached Burton Peak (2,020 feet) which is wooded with no view. Holt Peak, also wooded with no view, is a 30-minute walk from here, with a few good views along the way of Mount Monadnock and Peterborough to the west. If you've parked another car in the Miller State Park lot, it will take another hour and 15 minutes to reach it from Holt. If you haven't, set a turnaround time and enjoy again the cool woodland walk along Temple Mountain's wild side as you work your way back to the trailhead.

Sightseeing: If you have time, you may want to visit the Wales Preserve off Spring Road in Sharon. This 448-acre Nature Conservancy property features a boreal bog, majestic softwoods, ferns, wildflowers, and a series of small cascades along the Gridley River. To get there, return to the junction of Temple Road/Route 123. Drive south on Route 123 for 0.6 mile. Turn right on Jarmany Hill Road and continue for 2.7 miles where you will make a left turn onto Mill Road. Follow Mill Road 0.7 mile and make a right onto Spring Hill Road. Drive 0.1 mile on Spring Hill Road and park near a one-lane bridge. The trail begins a short distance further on the left.

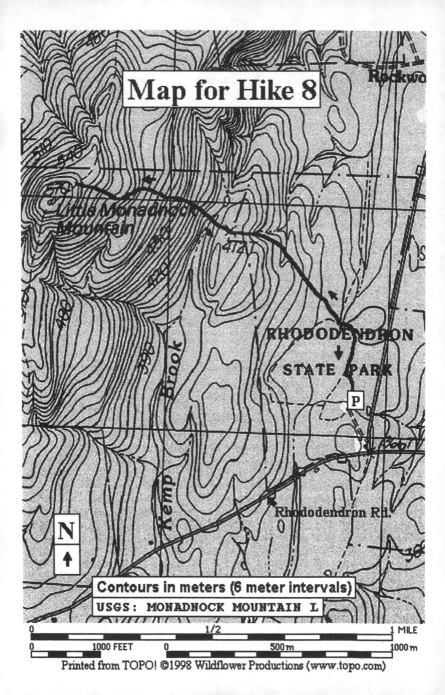

Map for Hike 8

Little Monadhock Mountain

RHODODENDRON

STATE PARK

P

Brook

Kemp

Rhododendron Rd.

N
↑

Contours in meters (6 meter intervals)

USGS: MONADNOCK MOUNTAIN L

| 0 | | 1/2 | | 1 MILE |

| 0 | 1000 FEET | 0 | 500 m | 1000 m |

Printed from TOPO! ©1998 Wildflower Productions (www.topo.com)

8

Little Monadnock Mountain

Rating: A moderate hike with some steep sections, through a state park with showy thickets of rhododendron, leading to a rocky promontory with fine views across a valley to Mount Monadnock and the Wapack Range.
Distance: 2.2 miles
Hiking time: 2 hours
Lowest Elevation: 1,200 feet
Highest elevation: 1,883 feet
USGS Map: Monadnock
Other Maps: AMC Metacomet-Monadnock Trail Guide

At slightly more than half the elevation and with only two trails leading to its 1,883-foot summit, Little Monadnock in Fitzwilliam doesn't come close to measuring up to the Grand Monadnock in size or reputation. But don't let this peak's anonymity discourage you from seeking it out. Little Monadnock is a gem waiting to step out of the shadow of her big sister and show her own sparkle: open ledge overlooks, a mind-boggling floral display, and a moderately paced two-mile hike you'll more than likely have all to yourself.

Designated a National Natural landmark in 1982, Rhododendron State Park features a 16-acre grove of *Rhododendron maximum* which is the northernmost native stand of wild Rhododendrons in New England. These magnificent leathery-leafed plants are in full bloom in mid-July, but more than 40 different varieties of wildflowers can be viewed all during the summer along the loop trails that skirt the natural bog area. Self-guided tour brochures are available at the park. A day-use fee is charged when the park is staffed.

Unusual double formation of paper birch

Access: From Keene, travel on Route 12 South to the Route 119 junction. Continue west on Route 119 to Fitzwilliam, a small community with a well kept, fenced common. One-half mile beyond this common, turn right onto Rhododendron Road which leads to the parking area and trailhead.

Description: The trail to Little Monadnock starts at the north end of the circular parking area to the left of a wooden bulletin board. After stepping between two rectangular stone pillars, the white-blazed markers direct you toward the *Rhododendron Loop Trail*. You'll walk past a picnic area in a shaded grove presided over by old-growth white pines taller than three-story tenement buildings. Neck craning is required to fully appreciate the beauty and stature of these giants.

Moments later you'll walk past rhododendron bushes; continue on the Rhododendron Loop Trail and then cross a wooden foot bridge. Just beyond this point the Rhododendron Loop Trail branches left. You'll continue to the right, walking through a mixed forest of hemlock, beech, maple, and pine. Here the path is matted with needles and oak leaves. This section of the hike is a pleasant woodland walk where you're likely to hear the tapping of a woodpecker digging its lunch from a decaying pine, or the sudden flutter of wings of a startled ruffed grouse. The trail will ascend gradually in a northerly direction past several boulders and two huge paper birch trees in the shape of a "Y." Just beyond this unusual tree formation, a sign informs you that you are leaving Rhododendron State Park.

After stepping between stone walls, you'll climb over a rocky outcrop and cross a stream on a crude pole bridge before encountering the most difficult stretch of the hike: an uphill climb over a boulder-strewn path that will test your lungs and legs for five minutes. The trail skirts the edge of the woods on a ledge of granite outcrop, giving you a momentary glimpse of Gap Mountain beyond a gnarled pine to the northeast, then levels out. At this point, a long stone wall parallels the trail to the right for several minutes as you walk uphill. After turning right and stepping between the stone wall, the path steepens again, but by the time you've had a chance to work up a sweat, you'll be near the top, standing on the northeast end of the summit ridge.

Little Monadnock's summit is a short distance above you to the left, but it is wooded with no view. Although the view from the ridge is good, take time to locate a large "MM" painted in white with an arrow pointing northeast. This is the Metacomet-Monadnock Trail, which is 117 miles long. It originates in Meriden, Connecticut, and ends at the summit of Mount Monadnock (eight miles away).

Follow the M-M Trail down the backbone of the ridge and into the woods for a few minutes to an open ledge area known as the North Meadows. Here the view opens up like a vast ocean. Nestled in the valley to the north is the quiet village of Troy, with its white-steepled town hall, Congregational church and landmark red brick smokestack chimney of the Troy Mills. Mount Monadnock's treeless summit and the notched ridgeline of Gap Mountain stand out prominently to the northeast, and like a long black fan, the Wapack Range unfolds to the southeast. The view to the Connecticut River Valley and Vermont is no less impressive, stretching like a rumpled blanket, with copper green, jade, and cobalt bumps dotting the glacially carved landscape as far as the eye can see. Take some time to enjoy the sounds you don't normally hear; the wind rustling in the trees, the shrill notes of mountain birds, or perhaps the muffled wail of a far-away factory whistle. When you are ready to return, re-enter the woods for the short walk back to Little Monadnock's summit ridge and descend to the park by retracing your route.

Sightseeing: The nearby town of Fitzwilliam is well worth investigating. The white-spired Town House, originally a

Congregational Church, is the centerpiece of the common. This handsome building burned in 1816 but was rebuilt in 1817. The bell survived the fire, but was later cracked in sounding an alarm. When it was later recast, 300 silver dollars were added to its metal in the belief that the tone would be improved. The three doors of the two story building are framed by a pedimented portico supported at each end by two pairs of Ionic columns. In the second story is a Palladian window. A four-storied steeple crowns the building, consisting of a square clock tower, belfry, and two octagonal lantern stages topped by a short spire and weathervane. The Fitzwilliam Museum at the Amos J. Blake House is located on the common and is open Saturdays 10-4 and Sundays 1-4, late May through mid-October.

View from Little Monadnock Mountain --
Mount Monadnock, Gap Mountain, and the Wapack Range

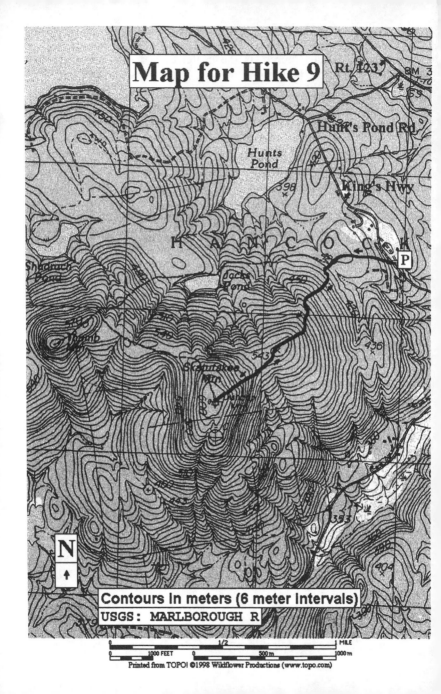

Map for Hike 9

Rt. 123

Hunt's Pond Rd.

Hunts Pond

King's Hwy

H A N C O C C K

Jacks Pond

P

Shadrack Pond

Skuttekee Mtn

N

Contours in meters (6 meter intervals)

USGS : MARLBOROUGH R

0   1/2   1 MILE

0   1000 FEET   0   500 m   1000 m

Printed from TOPO! ©1998 Wildflower Productions (www.topo.com)

9

Skatutakee Mountain

Rating: An easy-to-moderately steep climb to the summit of a 2,002-foot mountain with a striking view of Mount Monadnock and the Contoocook Valley
Distance: 3 miles
Hiking time: 2 hours
Lowest Elevation: 1,342 feet
Highest Elevation: 2,002 feet
USGS Map: Marlborough
Other Maps: Harris Center Trail map

You don't have to journey to the White Mountains to get spectacular views of the New Hampshire countryside. Less than an hour's drive from the Manchester/Nashua area stands Mount Skatutakee, a little-known mountain in Hancock with a big-time view. With its open views to the south, southeast, and southwest, Skatutakee is also an excellent spot to watch for migrating hawks. Make sure to pack a lunch as you'll want to spend some time on the 2,002-foot summit, and don't forget a canteen of water, which is not available on the trail.

Part of a nearly 8,500-acre "supersanctuary" block of land protected from development and open to the public's enjoyment, Mount Skatutakee is a gift of Eleanor Briggs who founded the Harris Center for Conservation Education in 1970. A non-profit organization dedicated to promoting the understanding and enjoyment of the outdoors, the Harris Center coordinates hikes and walks throughout the region and is respected for its conservation and wildlife management programs. The Harris Center's headquarters originally was a summer house built in the 1920s. Weekend programs range from mushroom identification and bird counts to forestry management and trail construction. Short interpretative trails are available on the property site. The Center's environmental education curriculum, which includes such programs as air and water quality monitoring projects, reaches 1,500 adults and more than 4,000 students in twenty seven private and public schools in southwestern New Hampshire each year.

Mount Skatutakee is located in Hancock, a classic New England town named after the man who was first to place his signature on the Declaration of Independence. Although he owned nearly 2000 acres of town land, John Hancock never set foot in this town. Across from the town green you'll find the First Congregation Church/Meeting House (1820) which is reputed to be the most photographed church in New England. This handsome white building has a pedimented main portal and a large Palladian window flanked by Ionic pilasters. In 1851 the building was moved to its present site from across the road and divided into two stories. The upper one is used as a church auditorium, and the lower one as the town hall. In the belfry is a Paul Revere Bell. Other local points of interest include the John Hancock Inn (1789), old cemetery, and the peaceful waters of Norway Pond across from the town common.

Access: To get to Skatutakee, take Route 123 North from the center of Hancock. After 2.5 miles, a sign will direct you left onto Hunt's Pond Road and the Harris Center. Go uphill for 0.4 mile, then turn left onto the King's Highway. The parking area is located to the rear of the Harris Center. The trailhead to Skatutakee enters the woods 0.1 mile beyond two stone entranceway posts to the Harris Center. (Walk down the dirt road to the right of the entranceway posts and look for a sign reading "Briggs Preserve" marked by the pawprint of a cat.)

Looking south from the summit of Skatutakee toward the Wapack Range

Description: The 1.5-mile-long Harriscat Trail was laid out in the summer of 1986 as a less strenuous alternative to the Beeline Trail, which begins at Old Dublin Road and was previously the only way to the summit. The first part of the trail is a pleasant walk through the woods past slender young maples poking through a green blanket of Canada mayflower. A few primeval white pines and the sun-dappled forest floor may elicit a Hansel and Gretel feeling. But the white rectangular blazes on nearly every other tree make it impossible to get lost on this trail.

Fifteen minutes into the hike, you'll maneuver through an area of huge boulders amid a boggy area. The trail rises gradually past a spur on the right, blazed in yellow triangles (this is the "Thumbs Down Trail" junction). Keep left as indicated by the white rectangles. At this point you'll notice the birch and maple trees begin to get larger with some spruce mixing in.

Five minutes later you'll step through the first of several stone walls on the way to the summit. Presently you'll walk over a "train" of boulders left behind by the glaciers and notice a huge beech tree to the right that looks like an elephant's leg stepping out of the forest into your path. A few more minutes uphill brings you to a wooden Harris Center sign pointing the opposite way. Here the trail takes a sharp right turn through a quiet stand of towering spruce and white pine trees. Fifty minutes on the trail will bring you to your first open view -- a ledge looking southeast to the tri-peaks of Crotched Mountain rising up majestically from the forest floor below you. The view of the twin peaks of the Uncanoonucs in Goffstown and Joe English Hill will tempt you to linger, but something even better is just ahead.

A five-minute scramble over outcrop covered with juniper and blueberry bushes separates you from the summit. Here you'll be surprised how suddenly the countryside opens up. The highlight of this vista is the broad, dark shoulders of Mount Monadnock, ruling the horizon across a wide valley to the west. This 3,165-foot giant never fails to inspire and the view from Skatutakee is one of the best. Crotched Mountain provides its own inspiration to the east. In between is the scenic 21-mile-long Wapack Range running along a ridgeline of mountains from North Pack Monadnock Mountain in Greenfield to Mount Watatic in Ashburnham, Massachusetts.

Sightseeing: If you have some extra time after enjoying lunch on the open ledges, you may want to explore Mount Thumb to the west of Skatutakee. For years it was inaccessible to hikers except by bush-whacking, but Mount Thumb can now be reached by using the Thumbs Up Trail (built in 1987). Blazed with white triangles, the trail descends Mount Skatutakee's upper slopes and across a saddle before ascending the 1,920-foot Thumb Mountain.

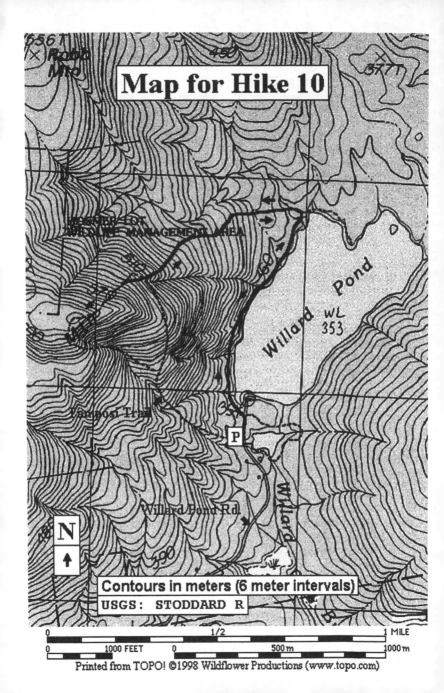

Map for Hike 10

Willard Pond

WL
353

HUBBARD LOT
WILDLIFE MANAGEMENT AREA

Campost Trail

P

Willard Pond Rd

N

Contours in meters (6 meter intervals)
USGS: STODDARD R

0   1/2   1 MILE
0   1000 FEET
0   500 m   1000 m

Printed from TOPO! ©1998 Wildflower Productions (www.topo.com)

10

Bald Mountain

Rating: A challenging hike along the edge of a wilderness pond to the ledgy summit of a 2,037-foot mountain with good views of the Wapack Range and Mount Monadnock, and options for extended hiking.
Distance: 2.2 miles
Hiking Time: 2 1/2 hours
Lowest Elevation: 1,158 feet (Willard Pond)
Highest Elevation: 2,037 feet
USGS Map: Stoddard
Other Maps: Audubon Society of New Hampshire trail guide

Bald Mountain in Antrim is part of the DePierrefeu-Willard Pond Wildlife Sanctuary, a 2,000-acre preserve protected by the Audubon Society of New Hampshire. The undeveloped tract includes hills, pristine ponds, and a mixture of woodlands that are home to coyotes, fox, porcupine, snowshoe hare, bobcat, deer, moose, and an occasional black bear. Also found here are fishers -- large members of the Mustellid family (mink, weasel) who feed on squirrels, hares, and porcupines. This is a prime birding location and nesting area for both the turkey vulture and raven. Because the area is a protected wildlife sanctuary, dogs are not allowed. Be sure to bring plenty of water as it is not available on the trail.

Access: To reach the trailhead from the Manchester area, take Route 101 West to Peterborough. Continue north on Route 123 to Hancock. From the village center, follow 123 North until you see a *Harris Center* sign. At 0.9 mile beyond the sign, turn right onto Davenport Road (dirt) which goes immediately downhill. Stay to the right of a triangle intersection with Willard Pond Road. About 0.2 mile beyond the intersection, you'll reach a small brown wooden shed which shelters a cluster of mailboxes. Stay left to follow Willard Pond Road past a yellow *Slow -- Children* sign. The parking lot is one mile beyond this point.

(Note: An important optional route, the Tamposi Trail, also starts from the parking lot. For the description of this option, see page 79.)

Description: From the parking lot, walk north up the dirt road that leads to Willard Pond. The trailhead (Tudor Trail) is located to the left in the woods about 100 yards beyond a caretaker's cottage. The first stretch of the hike is a pleasant 25-minute walk that skirts the western shoreline of Willard Pond to avoid the steep eastern flank of the mountain. Named for an old hunter who fished its waters and trapped on its shores, the 100-acre Willard Pond is cold and deep (80 feet in some places), somewhat similar to a high country lake. Swimming is allowed at your own risk.; the beach is small and secluded. Willard Pond is also a popular spot for canoeists and fishermen (fly fishing only). A mill pond at the outlet of Willard Pond was once the site of a saw and shingle mill which was later converted to a manufactory of bobbins, washboards, and clothespins.

[*Option:* There is a yellow-blazed trail here, a 15-minute walk that leads around the mill pond, which you may want to try out on your return trip from Bald Mountain.]

The trail to Bald Mountain is initially marked by yellow, rectangular metal blazes attached to trees. Make sure to stay to the right along the shoreline as this yellow trail loops back on itself. As you walk along the shoreline, you can't help but notice the abundance of large boulders strewn about the woods -- evidence of the glaciers' work thirteen thousand years ago. Beech, birch, maple, and some huge white pines are a counterpoint to the soft blanket of ferns, evergreen yew, clintonia, and a variety of mosses. Tree-shrouded coves studded with boulders will tempt you to sit for a while and contemplate the lake. Look for waterfowl who visit here, including woodducks, common loons and hooded mergansers.

Ten minutes into the hike, you will see a series of enormous boulders that seem to have tumbled out of the steeply sloped woods to the left. As you step through a maze of rocks here, the yellow, metal trail blazes change to red oblongs (second fork -- Bald Mountain Trail). Huge beech and birch trees dominate this section of the hike, and the gnawed trunks on the shoreline show evidence of beavers' work. You are likely to see coyote or raccoon skat or porcupine teeth markings on a beech tree. Bald Mountain was once a foraging ground for moose who abounded here. Shortly you'll reach a plank bridge that crosses an unmoving stream. As the trail turns westward and uphill into the woods, you will be dwarfed by more boulders, some the size of small houses, with their flat surfaces cloaked in green. From here it is about a half-hour walk to the top.

Bald Mountain from across Hatch Mill Pond

[*Option:* Just after the big boulders, the Pine Point Trail to your right leads to a pond overlook. Taking this adds another ten minutes to your walk.]

From the boulders, the last section of the Bald Mountain Trail is moderately strenuous and steep. After ten minutes, you'll step through a gap in a stone wall and continue past a grove of bushy striped maples and a thickly wooded stretch before distant mountain views begin to open up. Soon you'll reach the yellow-blazed Tamposi Trail junction. The trail continues through a red spruce forest before joining the Tamposi Trail for the final stretch to the top, above the rock cliff ledge. As with many other peaks with the same name, the "baldness" is the result of a forest fire.

View from Bald Mountain

Impressive Mount Monadnock dominates the horizon to the southwest. The expansive sheet of water in the foreground, three miles to the southwest, is Lake Nubanusit, which is connected to Spoonwood Pond. Skatutakee and Thumb Mountains rise behind Spoonwood Pond. Directly south, ribbons of marsh curve like silver snakes against the backdrop of the Wapack Range. Further east lie the Lyndeborough Mountains and Crotched Mountain. The Uncanoonuc Mountains in Goffstown are visible in the distance behind Crotched. Willard Pond sparkles like an emerald jewel directly below you with Goodhue Hill rising behind it.

The blueberry and juniper covered ledges invite you to sit and have lunch and soak in the solitude. When you are ready to return, walk eastward and follow the same route back to the parking lot. (An alternate route is to take the yellow-blazed Tamposi Trail. From the summit, the Tamposi Trail continues into a spruce forest and down the south side of the mountain to the parking lot.) If you have time, you may want to follow the Mill Pond Trail. This 15-minute loop begins opposite the Tutor Trail sign and leads past a beaver lodge, old dam site, and interesting trough-like formation of stones.

Tamposi Trail Option: The yellow-blazed Tamposi Trail leaves the back corner of the parking lot. Walking time for the 2.2-mile moderate loop is 1.5 hours. Markers encourage walking in a counter-clockwise direction (more difficult going up; easier coming down). A moderate slope is maintained by switchbacks in the steep sections. The trail starts uphill through a beech and red oak forest. Soon you'll walk past a field of large boulders broken off from the top of Bald Mountain as ice moved southeast during the last Ice Age. Many of the giant rocks lie scattered in tunnel and cave formations which kids and adults will want to explore. You'll see Rock Tripe lichen here, attached to the rocky surfaces like leathery dark lettuce leaves.

After squeezing through a narrow opening between two boulders, the trail continues uphill past a stone wall to the right. Soon you'll get a glimpse of Willard Pond 600 feet below you. Twenty minutes from the start of the hike, you'll reach an expansive ledge-outcrop area with ample room for stretching out. This is the highlight of the hike, and you'll want to spend time taking in the spectacular view of Willard Pond and surrounding mountains from the top of the ledges.

From the ledge area, the trail continues uphill and shortly intersects with the (red) Bald Mountain Trail. A steep section brings you through a red spruce forest. Soon you'll emerge from the trees at an open ledge. A few minutes more of walking brings you to the summit. From the top, the Tamposi Trail continues into a 100-year-old spruce forest. A sign here indicates that it is 1.1 miles to the parking lot. The trail continues downhill past meadows and turns right to move past the boulders and back to the parking lot.

11

North Pack Monadnock

Rating: A moderate climb up the north face of the anchoring mountain of the Wapack Range. Ledgy outcrops offer expansive views along the way, and from the summit there is a sweeping view of the Wapack Range and Mount Monadnock.
Distance: 3 miles
Hiking time: 2 hours
Lowest Elevation: 1,314 feet
Highest Elevation: 2,276 feet
USGS Map: Greenfield
Other Maps: Wapack Trail Guide and Map, New Hampshire Division of Parks and Recreation map.

North Pack Monadnock Mountain is certainly not as well known as the 3,165-foot Mt. Monadnock to the southwest. It even pales in comparison to its sister peak, South Pack Monadnock Mountain in Peterborough, which boasts a scenic 1.3-mile auto road leading to Miller State Park on its windswept summit. But taking the 1.5-mile trail to the 2,278-foot summit of North Pack provides equally rewarding vistas and a quiet retreat. If you are seeking an easy-to-moderate climb, North Pack Monadnock Mountain is well worth the hour's effort it takes to reach the top.

Actually, North Pack is just one of many mountains in southwestern New Hampshire which geologists call "monadnocks." These isolated hills rise above the rolling terrain as masses of durable rock that resisted the erosion of the surrounding land. Getting to one of these isolated peaks requires an hour's drive from the Manchester/Nashua area. In many ways, the long sweeping views here are superior to the vistas of the more crowded summits to the north.

You will be hiking the final leg of the Wapack trail, a 21-mile-long string of monadnocks extending northward from Mount Watatic in Ashburnham, Massachusetts, to its terminus at North Pack. Well marked by yellow triangles painted on trees and rocks, the trail will carry you through quiet forest glens, abandoned farm pastures, and along open ledges and summits marked by cairns.

The Wapack National Wildlife Refuge (1,672 acres) is a major portion of North Pack. It is mostly a timbered area, containing a swamp, bog, and bare rock ledge and cliff area. A valuable habitat for upland wildlife and important hawk migration flyway, it also provides a nesting area for tree sparrows, winter wrens, pine grosbeaks, cedar waxwings, and thrush and warbler species. Camping and open fires are prohibited. The refuge is administered from Great Meadows National Wildlife Refuge in Sudbury, Massachusetts.

Access: *North approach.* To get to the trailhead from the Manchester area, take Route 114 West to Route 13 South in Goffstown. Follow Route 13 as it wends its way alongside the South Branch of the Piscataquog River for 7 miles to New Boston. Then travel Route 136 West for 12 miles to Greenfield. At a blinking light, take Route 31 South for approximately 2.8 miles before turning right onto Russell Station Road. The landmark to watch for is the Yankee Farmer, an outdoor farmstand. Wapack trail maps and information are available here. After turning onto Russell Station Road, you'll drive over a set of railroad tracks and past an intersecting dirt road before coming to Mountain Road. Turn right onto Mountain Road. Continue driving uphill past a gray colonial house with red trim, a farm, and an unusual house made of fieldstone. The trailhead is 0.9 mile beyond this point. Park your car on the shoulder of the road and look for a yellow triangle blaze on a maple tree and Wapack trail sign.

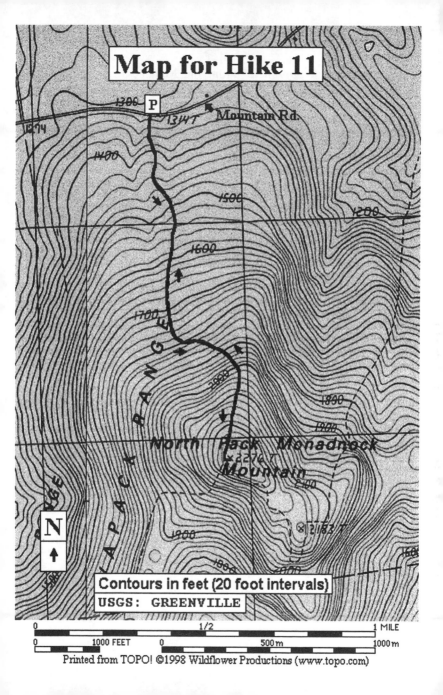

Map for Hike 11

P

1300

1274

1400

1314T Mountain Rd.

1500

1200

1600

1700

R
A
N
G
E

1800

1900

1800

1900

K
A
P
A
C
A
North Pack Monadnock

2276T Mountain

2400

1900

⊗ 2183 T

N
↑

1800

1800

1800

2000

1600

Contours in feet (20 foot intervals)
USGS: GREENVILLE

0   1/2   1 MILE
0   1000 FEET   0   500 m   1000 m

Printed from TOPO! ©1998 Wildflower Productions (www.topo.com)

Access South approach: From the Manchester area, take Route 101 West to Wilton. From the center of town, continue north on Route 31 for 7.9 miles to Russell Station Road.

Description: The sign at the trailhead informs you that it is 1.5 miles to the summit of North Pack. Early on, the hiking is easy but be wary of tentacle-like roots that are tangled across the trail. You'll travel through a corridor of huge white pine, many of them dead and decaying, their skeleton branches looking like eerie silhouettes among the growth of young trees mixing in.

After five minutes, the trail winds through a stone wall, then descends into a grove of young maples. A stream splashes on your left, the first of several watercourses traversing your path. According to the AMC Guide, there is a spring of reliable drinking water halfway up the mountain. Shortly after crossing the stream you'll walk through an impressive display of mountain laurel growing on both sides of the trail.

One half hour on the trail brings you to the halfway point. You'll climb hand over foot for a short stretch over a jumble of huge boulders and flat sloping rocks, then walk past several small cairns before stepping out onto a series of wide, flat open ledges for your first open view. Directly behind you to the north, glinting in the sunlight, is the cluster of buildings that comprise the Crotched Mountain Rehabilitation Center. The village of Greenfield is in the valley below, while the rounded summits of Winn, Lyndeborough, and Rose Mountains rise gently to the east. In between these are the Uncanoonucs in Goffstown, and beyond them the city of Manchester.

Many hikers choose to end their walk here; you will often see people sunning themselves on the rocks. But after you've caught your breath and perhaps refreshed yourself with a snack and drink of water, head back on the trail which continues up over a series of granite ledges worn smooth by the glaciers and flanked by spreading shrubs of juniper. There's a good chance you'll hear the hoarse whistle of a red-tailed hawk adrift in the summer sky. The trail alternately travels up over granite outcrop, then disappears into a spruce and hardwood forest. In 15 minutes, you'll come to what looks like a dry stream bed to the right of the trail. Be sure to stay to the left, noting the yellow blaze on a tree and two small cairns, which will guide you back on your return trip. From this point, a 10-minute walk through a quiet spruce forest is all that separates you from the summit. A six-foot stone cairn announces the end of your hike. Just to the west of this marker, the Wapack Trail leaves the ledges and continues 2.2 miles south to Pack Monadnock Mountain.

From where you are standing, you can see Pack Monadnock's lookout tower, microwave dish antennae and communications towers. Toward the southwest, Temple, Kidder, and Barrett Mountains stretch to Mount Watatic in Massachusetts on the horizon. Mount Monadnock in all its glory stands out prominently to the west. According to the AMC Guide, views of the Contoocook River Valley, Mount Washington, and other White Mountain peaks are visible to the north on a clear day. A short walk to the east of the summit cairn brings you to an exposed rock outlook and an unusual view of two white objects that look like gigantic golf balls. These are spotting towers of a United States Air Force satellite tracking station in New Boston just southeast of Joe English Hill. Back at the summit cairn, a blue trail leads to a cliff outlook on the southeast side of North Pack. When you've soaked in enough of the scenery, walk north and look for the yellow-blazed return trail entering the spruce forest.

Option: Ted's Trail is a 6-mile loop trail from Mountain Road to North Pack's 2,276-foot summit and back. The yellow-blazed route takes you past a waterfall, moves through hemlock, beech and spruce forests, and offers good views to the east, northeast and south. The trailhead is located off Mountain Road 0.5 mile from the junction of Russell Station and Mountain Road.

View of Mount Monadnock from North Pack

12

Pack Monadnock Mountain

Rating: Moderate. A loop hike that follows the Wapack Trail to the summit and returns via the Marion Davis Trail. There are ledgy uphill sections and good views of the Contoocook River Valley along the way.
Distance: 2.8 miles
Hiking time: 2 hours
Lowest Elevation: 1,485 feet
Highest Elevation: 2,290 feet
USGS Map: Peterborough South
Other Maps: New Hampshire Division of Parks and Recreation Map, Wapack Trail Guide and Map.

For over one hundred years, Miller State Park on the summit of Pack Monadnock Mountain in Peterborough has been a popular spot to enjoy a picnic, watch hawks wing their way along their migratory routes, or savor the view of the Souhegan River Valley from the 27-foot lookout tower. Along with three foot trails, there is a 1.3-mile paved switchback road that climbs to the top. The loop hike outlined here takes you up the 2,290-foot mountain on a yellow-blazed 1.4-mile section of the Wapack Trail, with the return route via the blue-blazed 1.4-mile Marion Davis Trail. The Wapack Trail is a 21-mile-long footpath, the first interstate hiking trail in the United States, which runs from Mount Watatic in Ashburnham, Massachusetts, to North Pack Monadnock Mountain in Greenfield, New Hampshire.

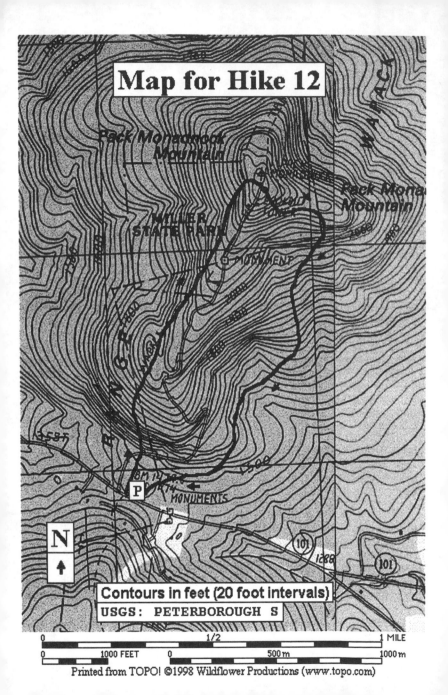

Map for Hike 12

Pack Monadnock Mountain

MILLER STATE PARK

MONUMENT

Pack Mona Mountain

P

MONUMENTS

101

101

N

Contours in feet (20 foot intervals)
USGS: PETERBOROUGH S

0 · · 1/2 · · 1 MILE

0 · 1000 FEET · 0 · 500 m · 1000 m

Printed from TOPO! ©1998 Wildflower Productions (www.topo.com)

The oldest park in the New Hampshire system, Miller State Park is an especially busy place in the fall on weekends. It is not uncommon for cars to be backed up for an hour's wait to drive to the top. Dogs are allowed, but must be leashed, and the park is staffed until November. For more information contact the New Hampshire Division of Parks and Recreation, PO Box 1856, Concord, NH 03302-1856.

The summit of Pack Monadnock Mountain is a favorite picnic spot for families who love to hike

The park brochure states that the name "Pack" comes from a Native American word meaning little. Others believe that "pack" was a misspelling by a draftsman or engraver of an early map, perhaps for a family named Packer who owned and farmed land on the mountain. Another reason has to do with the Pack Monadnock Range resembling a "pack of wolves."

Access:. To get to Miller State Park on Pack Monadnock from the Manchester area, take Route 101 West to the Temple Mountain Ski Area in Peterborough gap. The entrance to the park is just west of the ski area. The foot trails area is located a short distance east of a large brown wooden information sign and toll station in the parking lot. In season (April to November), a $2.50 fee is charged to hike the trails or drive to the top (New Hampshire residents over 65 and under 12 enter for free). The yellow Wapack Trail starts to the left (northeast) of a glassed-in bulletin board displaying a map of the entire Wapack Trail. Dogs are allowed. For information, call the toll station at 603-924-3672.

Description: The hike begins in a mixed forest of maple, spruce, and oak, where you will see Canada Mayflower (the wild lily-of-the-valley), the first bitter green to appear on the forest floor in spring. Canada Mayflower grows in masses that cover the ground with shining leaves, heart-shaped at the base. A spike of fine white flowers is borne erect on a single stem, followed by a cluster of berries. In late summer the green berries of Canada Mayflower turn to pinkish-beige, and in fall change again to red. Shortly the trail crosses the auto road, then re-enters the woods to ascend a steep ridge with difficult footing over rough slabs of schist.

In the late summer acorns spring from leafy oaks, and scallop-like cliffs of fractured ledge provide an interesting natural sculpture. Although this stretch may not demand the physical exertion of some of the White Mountain hikes, it is nonetheless a knee-lifter which explains why the contour lines are bunched together on a topographical map.

After you pass beneath a power line, some fine views of Temple Mountain and its ski trails begin to show to the southwest. Twisted birch trees literally sprout from the rocky ledge like weeds pushing up between flagstone walkways, making the maximum use of the limited soil at their base. Minutes later a great view of Mount Monadnock will stop you dead in your tracks. Take time to walk a few steps off the trail for an even better view -- to a flat rock overlook marked by several semi-circular balcony-like rock walls, many of them pushed over. The ledgy footing alternates with scrub woods and brush as you continue to climb. Far below you to the left, Route 101 winds it way westward through the forested valley and past Cunningham Pond.

As you continue, you'll appreciate the trailwork done by the *Friends of the Wapack* -- a volunteer group that clears brush, tree limbs and blowdowns, helping to preserve the well-blazed path. About one-half hour into the hike will bring you to an old pasture overtaken by juniper. Like many hills and mountains of the Monadnock region, the slopes of Pack were once open fields and pastures where cattle driven up from farms in Massachusetts grazed during the summer. After passing several misshapen beech trees, the trail descends into a gully where, in late summer and early fall, clusters of daisy-like wood aster grow alongside the dry stream bed. As you enter the 2000-foot elevation zone, spruce trees become more evident, as do the bright red bunchberry, clintonia, wood sorrel, and ferns.

Ten minutes later you'll step through an opening in a stone wall to enter a dense spruce forest with broken and dying lower tree limbs. You might hear the sound of cars off to the right, and you'll continue for 15 minutes to a small intermittent brook crossing. After a few minutes the trail intersects the Summit Loop Trail. Continue right for the short walk to the summit. At the top you'll find a ranger shed, parking lot, observation tower with stick antennae and micro-wave discs, picnic tables, water bubblers (from a 300-foot-deep spring-fed well), fireplaces, pit toilets, and a three-sided stone shelter. The Wapack Trail continues from the summit to North Pack Monadnock Mountain (2.3 miles).

View of the Wapack Range from South Pack Monadnock

Chances are that you'll have lots of company at the top because Pack Monadnock has always been a mecca for humans. At the turn of the century, many families in nearby Temple profited from the boarding house and hotel trade when "summer people" nearly doubled the town's population. After morning chores, the farm owner would drive his guests to Pack Monadnock and Miller State Park where they would enjoy lunches packed in round wooden cheese boxes, gallon jugs and two-gallon milk cans, returning in the afternoon in time for the owner to begin his evening chores.

The summer people also enjoyed one of Temple's most acclaimed spots -- the Pack Monadnock Lithia Springs owned by Sidney Scammon. Scammon bottled and sold the water, proclaiming that it was the most wonderful natural spring water known in the world. For twenty years people from miles around came to seek out the curative powers of the spring as a remedy for kidney trouble, rheumatism, Bright's disease, eczema, indigestion, and dyspepsia. The Site also gained renown as a popular recreation and picnic grove. In 1911, however, Scammon was caught mixing a batch of lithium in the spring. When news of the deception got out, the crafty entrepreneur beat a hasty retreat to Malden, Massachusetts. Shortly afterwards, a portable lumber sawmill company bought the property and removed the grove of great pines. Temple's most acclaimed landmark was no more.

Today the remnants of Lithia Springs can be found at the end of a dirt road (Lithia Springs Road), 1.8 miles west of the village of Temple. (To get there from Miller State Park, travel on Route 101 east for 1.9 miles to Route 45 South. Continue on Route 45 for 0.1 mile to Lithia Springs Road.)

Pack Monadnock even had its own hotel once, the Pioneer House, a rambling two-story structure built on the southwest shoulder with a reputation for its uncluttered vista and healthy mountain air. Unfortunately it burned to the ground in 1896. A new structure replaced it and was used as a hunting lodge, but was later abandoned and fell into disrepair; then was leveled by fire in 1924. You can still see remnants of the cellar hole by following the auto road 0.6 mile down from the top of the mountain. Just below the hairpin turn, look for a chain stretched across the turnoff road to the right. Walk up the road past a chain link fenced-in area -- this is leased by MIT and is used as a transmitter site to evaluate the performance of their communication antennae in Westford, Massachusetts. The cellar hole is just beyond the fenced-in area.

The summit continues to be a popular place to picnic, and is the site of an occasional wedding and meeting place for ham radio operators. The view from the 27-foot-tall tower is a spectacular 360 degrees.

The mountains that are easily distinguishable include Temple to the south; the Wapack Range to the southwest; Mount Monadnock (12 miles away), Gap Mountain, Little Monadnock Mountain, Stratton Mountain in Vermont to the west and Killington farther north. North Pack (directly in the foreground), Crotched, and Kearsarge (behind Crotched) can be seen to the north. To the northeast lie the Lyndeborough Mountains, Joe English Hill, and the radome of the Air Force Satellite Tracking station in New Boston, which looks like a giant white golfball. To the right of the tracking station you can see the brick buildings of the city of Manchester sprawling in the valley. To the distant northeast lie Saddleback Mountain and the double-bumped Pawtuckaway Mountains in Nottingham, New Hampshire. Cardigan Mountain lies northwest, with Mount Ascutney in Vermont a little more to the west of Cardigan. The large body of water to the southeast is the Greenville Reservoir, and to the west are Cranberry Meadow and Cunningham Ponds in Peterborough.

On a clear day in fall or late spring, you can see white-capped Mount Washington in the distant north, 100 miles away. It is visible on the horizon just off the left shoulder of North Pack Monadnock Mountain in the foreground. Follow the distant ridge slowly with your gaze. You will see two bumps. The next prominent bump in the background (hazier blue, it almost looks like a cloud) behind the ridge is Mount Washington. Have patience, it takes a steady eye to see it. The city of Boston is visible 55 miles away to the southeast. The Prudential and Hancock buildings stand by themselves to the right of the cluster of buildings comprising the Boston skyline. A different perspective of the same view may be obtained by following the Summit Loop Trail (red circles), which leads to several good outlooks. The trail begins just to the north (left) of the ranger cabin.

Take some time to enjoy lunch and the show put on by nature. In July dragonflies buzz around the summit like squadrons of miniature helicopters. White-throated Sparrows, Juncos and Towhees are some of the common mountain birds you'll see and hear. In mid-September you're apt to catch the Audubon Society of New Hampshire monitoring the fall hawk migration. The Wapack Range is a leading line for hawks seeking wind currents to ride. Hawks fly by day, riding the rising heat columns (thermals) or the currents along the ridgeline. Thermals form over areas that absorb the sun's energy, such as the slopes of mountains, plowed fields, and large expanses of pavement.

The hawks most often seen are of the genus *buteo,* a group of large soaring hawks with broad, rounded wings and short tails spread out like a fan, a design well-suited for exploiting the lifting power of winds and thermals. It's possible to see Peregrine falcons or duck hawks, probably the rarest of North American hawks.

You might also spot robin-sized kestrels, or sparrow hawks, northern harriers (with their telltale white rump-patch), ravens, and turkey vultures (easily recognizable because their wings tip upward in a "V" shape). Other possible sightings are sharp-shinned hawks (about the size of a blue jay, with their hallmark quick flaps and longer glide), osprey, Bald Eagles, Cooper's, red-tailed, red-shouldered, northern goshawks, and broadwings, with their conspicuous white and brown banded tails, the first to leave for the warmer climes and who make up the greater numbers.

After you've enjoyed the sights, walk to the green park shed with the water fountain on the corner. From here you should see the sign and blue trail blazes for the Marion Davis Trail. This trail is named for Marion Davis, a rugged outdoors woman and champion rail splitter, who helped to establish and maintain the Wapack Trail during its early years. Davis and her husband later (1925) built the Wapack Lodge, a two-story structure that accommodated up to 25 overnight guests, on New Hampshire Route 123/124 in New Ipswich. (see **Hike # 2**, Kidder Mountain). Davis herself provided the hikers with hearty home cooked meals. The lodge closed in 1958 and it fell into disrepair. In July of 1993 it was struck by lightning and burned.

Although strewn with boulders, the Marion Davis Trail traverses less strenuous terrain than the Wapack Trail. On the 1.4 mile route back to the parking lot, you will pass airy, wooded dells and soft spoken streams along the way.

13

Greenfield-French Roads

Rating: An easy woodland walk down old town roads that will carry you past cellar holes, an old burial plot, and long forgotten stone walls.
Distance: 3 miles
Hiking Time: 2.5 hours
Lowest Elevation: 830 feet
Highest Elevation: 1000 feet
USGS Map: Greenfield

There's something special about walking down old town roads like the Greenfield and French Roads in Lyndeborough. They can give you the feeling that you're alone yet somehow connected to those who have traveled this way before. There are secrets here among the winding stone walls and cellar holes, and the stillness of the surrounding woodland offers opportunity for reflection. Located in the northwest corner of the town, the hike outlined here traces these old thoroughfares to the New Boston Road in Greenfield and back for a three-mile round trip. Depending on your thirst for exploration, you can complete the route in a few casual hours and return to your everyday world with a renewed appreciation for the past.

Access: To get to the trailhead from Manchester, Take NH 101 West to Wilton. From the Wilton traffic island drive north on NH 31 for 3.6 miles to South Lyndeborough. One-half mile beyond The Village Store, turn right onto Center Road. At 2.5 miles, turn left onto (Old) Mountain Road. After driving 2.5 miles you'll come to the French Road on the left. (This is where you would end the optional extension hike listed on page 103.) Continue for 0.7 mile (the road turns to a dirt surface), and park in a grassy clearing (left) near a telephone pole and red and white sign (*Road Closed -- Subject to Bars and Gates*). A small brown barn sits in a field across the road from the clearing. Make sure to pull your vehicle well off the road so as not to impede traffic, and please notice that much of the property along the way is posted, so be respectful of landowners.

Description: The trail starts out on the old Greenfield Road. Generally, old town roads have stone walls to either side and that is the case here. (Note: The first 0.6 mile of Greenfield Road has been widened and graded because of a logging operation.) You'll immediately walk downhill (northwest) past a residence on the left. The branches of enormous beech, birch, and maple trees enfold the trail in an impressive canopy above you, while ferns along the roadside put on their own brilliant display of rich greens. After crossing a small brook, you'll notice a clearing of logging activity at a break in the stone wall on the left. Look opposite in the woods to the right for an old foundation made of smooth-sided slabs of cut granite (upon close inspection you can see drill holes), with several white birch trees growing out of it.

Lyndeborough has a good number of old cellar holes like this one. Town histories report that many of the nineteenth century settlers abandoned the stony soil of New England to settle in the Midwest where there was deep, fertile soil. This particular cellar hole is all that remains of an old school house which has long since rotted away. Take time to step inside and look around. You can see a square formation of stone of what once was a chimney. A little further down the trail, look in the woods to the right again for another old cellar hole with a gnarled yellow birch tree growing out of it.

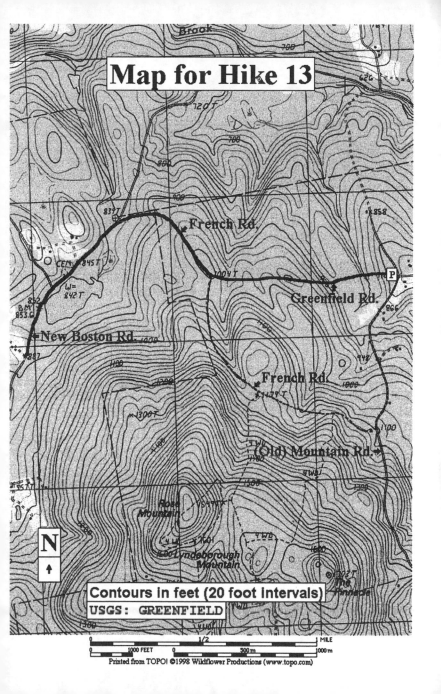

Map for Hike 13

French Rd.

P

Greenfield Rd.

New Boston Rd.

French Rd.

(Old) Mountain Rd.

Rose Mountain

Lyndeborough Mountain

The Pinnacle

N

↑

Contours in feet (20 foot Intervals)

USGS: GREENFIELD

| 0 | 1/2 | 1 MILE |
| 0 | 1000 FEET | 0 | 500 m | 1000 m |

Printed from TOPO! ©1998 Wildflower Productions (www.topo.com)

Old Greenfield-French Road

The trail continues through a red maple swamp -- ablaze in the autumn, buggy in the summer. You'll move abruptly up-hill through a grove of feathery hemlocks, and five minutes later the road levels out. Look to the right. In a clearing at a break in the stone wall beneath maple trees, the remains of old foundations for farm buildings slump in a depression in the forest floor, built of stones fitted together without mortar, now mossy and gray-green. Maple trees and a big mound of earth rise through spaces where early settlers once lived. In between the foundations is a large pile of stones covering an old well.

At 0.6 mile, the feel of the road changes to a country lane. You will pass through a grove of hemlocks and hardwoods bulging with odd shaped burls, then the road descends to cross two brooks. A beautiful display of hobble-bush is here in the spring, showing off its lacy white clusters of flowers in May. You will then come to a "Y" junction with the French Road. Turn right and north. Originally the main road to Francestown, the French Road today serves only as a thoroughfare for wildlife -- even moose tracks have been seen here in winter. Stone walls continue to follow you to either side and to the right is an area overgrown by juniper indicating an old pasture. Just beyond an intersecting tote road on the right, the French Road begins a gradual decline. In five minutes you'll come to a fork. Stay to the left to follow the badly eroded road downhill. At this point the towns of Lyndeborough, Francestown, and Greenfield come together, although there is no sign indicating the boundaries. The road levels out and moves over a wet area as the forest canopy begins to open up.

Minutes later you'll come to a junction with the hard-packed dirt New Boston Road. Continue left and southwest on the New Boston Road. French Road continues northwest across the New Boston Road along with another woods road. Follow the New Boston Road downhill past a marshy area, and a culvert channels a brook under the road, where you may spy a stilt-legged blue heron stalking its dinner. Otter have been seen here, too. Soon you'll see an old graveyard on the right, sitting on a moss-covered hill behind some tall white pines, a rusted gate, and stone wall. This is the Whittemore family cemetery and it makes an interesting and peaceful place to spend a few minutes. Major Amos Whittemore, who fought in the Battle of White Plains during the Revolution, is credited with naming the town of Greenfield. A stately federal brick home built by the Major still stands on the crest of a small hill a few hundred yards behind the cemetery at the end of a long dirt driveway and across from a field crisscrossed by stone walls.

The gravestones here are weather worn and some are difficult to read. Slate was the marker stone most used in the 1700s, until the advent of the railroads made it easier to ship granite. Some of the stone markers have rounded tops, others are arched or even edged with etchings of hands pointed skyward, elaborate willow trees (symbol of bereavement) bending over urns and winged angels. The burial urn and willow tree motif became popular during the 1800s and replaced the winged effigy which represents spiritual uplifting. Other symbol motifs included arches, crowns, doves, flowers, vases, and grapevines.

From the cemetery, the New Boston Road continues past a pond brimming with water lilies and Rose Mountain rising behind it. Walk down to the shoreline and you may surprise a female Mallard. 0.1 mile beyond the cemetery, the road changes to a tarred surface. This is the turn-around point of the hike. (From this point the New Boston Road continues west 2.3 miles to NH 31 in Greenfield.) Return to your car by the same route. Make sure to look for the French Road fork on the right at the crest of a small rise on the New Boston

Road 0.3 mile beyond the cemetery. Retrace your path back to the Greenfield Road junction and turn left for the fifteen minute walk back to your car.

Optional extension: You can bypass the Greenfield Road junction and continue straight and south on the French Road. Bear left at a fork at the top of a hill. A 25-minute walk will bring you back to Old Mountain Road. Along the way you'll see a large cellar hole on the left side of the road which marks the residence of the French family for whom the road was named. Just beyond the French family cellar hole, at the bottom of the hill, look in the woods to the left for the remains of an old soapstone quarry. You can see the indentations where they dug into the ground to mine soapstone, a soft rock composed mostly of mineral talc that is a good electric insulator. Soapstone is not affected by high temperatures. Years ago it was used to make sinks, table tops, stoves, and bed warmers. When you reach old Mountain Road, turn left and walk 0.7 mile on the tarred and dirt surface back to your car in the grassy clearing.

Sightseeing: If you have time, you may want to visit the sleepy hilltop community of Lyndeborough Center and view an interesting grave site and stone monument along the way. To get to Lyndeborough Center, return to Center Road, turn left and drive for 0.5 mile. One-tenth mile before Center Road, turn right onto Crooked S Road to visit the solitary tombstone marking the grave of Dr. Lorenzo D. Bartlett. Bartlett came to Lyndeborough in 1854 to minister to a young woman named Ann Jones and a small child who had contracted smallpox. Although his treatment was successful, Bartlett himself contracted the dreaded disease and died at the age of 29. So fearful were the people that the sickness would spread, they insisted he not be interred in the town cemetery. The grave site is located 0.4 mile down Crooked S Road on the right side under a cluster of oak trees.

Lyndeborough Cemetery

Before the railroad came through in 1870, Lyndeborough Center had a post office, store, dance hall, and tavern. Today, only the old town hall and United Church remain. Across a field from the church, look for the gentle slope of Piscataquog Mountain. Legend has it that silver was once mined on the ledges here and that one pair of buckles was fashioned from the precious metal. Just beyond the town hall, you'll find the Center Cemetery behind a white picket gate flanked by granite posts. Beyond the cemetery to the west is a spectacular view of Winn Mountain and the Pack Monadnocks.

Sightseeing: If you have time before or after your hike, there are many opportunities for sightseeing in the neighboring area of Wilton, a hillside town nestled on the banks of the Souhegan River. In years past it was a busy manufacturing village, at various times boasting cotton worsted yarn, cloth mills, woodworking plant, box factory, machine shop, and boot and shoe-making businesses. The granite building stone and under-pinning were cut out of the ledge along the Souhegan River. In the town center you'll find the fortress-like town hall of granite and brick, a sophisticated example of Queen Anne architecture with a monumental domed clock tower. This impressive building houses a movie theater in addition to town offices. Nearby are the Masonic Temple and the Gregg Free Library with a rotunda of Sienna marble, paneled throughout its interior with fine woods -- curly whitewood, sycamore, and mahogany.

Three miles north of Wilton you'll find Frye's Measure Mill, a manufacturer of wooden ware, colonial and shaker boxes, which is listed in the National Register of Historic Places. The museum shop offers a variety of hand-crafted products that are authentic survivors of 19th century technology and craftsmanship. They have been made in the same mill, and with the same machinery, still partially water powered, since 1858. In the older days the owners used a one-cylinder steam engine for additional power and to heat the mill, kilns, and steam vats. The engine still remains at the mill. It was made in Cambridgeport, Massachusetts in 1871 and its main flywheel measures six feet in diameter. The engine also powered the sawmill, which was removed a few years ago. To get to Frye's, drive north on Route 31 (Forest Road) for 1.5 miles to the Burton Highway. Fork left here and continue for another 1.5 miles.

Nearby also is Barnes (Gaerwin) Falls, a beautiful waterfall on County Farm Brook. Gaerwin Falls was the site of the first mill in Wilton, and a popular spot for picnics, church parties, outings, and school reunions. You can see many pot holes and basins worn in the ledges. To get to the Gaerwin Falls, turn left on the Isaac Frye Highway, 0.5 mile from the junction of Route 31 and Burton Highway. Continue driving on the Isaac Frye Highway for 0.5 mile. Just after a small bridge and Putnam Hill Road, look left for a woods road where a cable is stretched across the road. Park on the shoulder of the highway. A five minute walk down the woods road past the old Wilton Reservoir brings you to the head of the falls. Along the way you'll see tall pines, mountain laurel, and hemlock which grows in cool, moist ravines and likes the north side of hills facing rain-bearing winds.

Wilton Center lies one mile farther on the Isaac Frye Highway. It is a small village of beautiful homes, a small brick Federal-style Baptist church, Town Hall, Unitarian Church, and the "Yellow House," an excellent example of country Federal architecture.

Waterfall at Frye's Measure Mill, Wilton NH

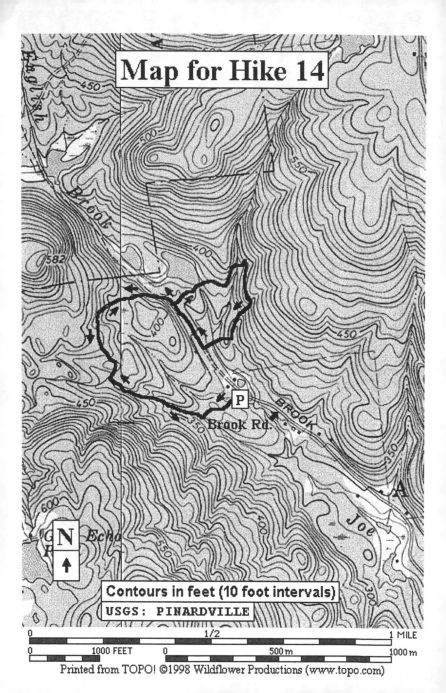

Map for Hike 14

English Brook

582

500

450

400

400

450

400

450

350

BROOK

P

Brook Rd.

550

550

600

Echo

Joe

300

N

Contours in feet (10 foot intervals)

USGS: PINARDVILLE

0   1/2   1 MILE

0   1000 FEET   0   500 m   1000 m

Printed from TOPO! ©1998 Wildflower Productions (www.topo.com)

14

Joe English Reservation

Rating: An easy loop hike through evergreen and deciduous woodland to a beaver pond, with a chance to discover a wild garden of plants, as well as the deer, fox, and other animals who make their homes here.
Distance: 2.25 miles
Hiking time: 1.5 hours
Lowest Elevation: 350 feet
Highest Elevation: 400 feet
USGS Map: Pinardville
Other Maps: Amherst Conservation Commission map

Joe English Reservation is located only 20 minutes from the bustle of downtown Manchester. Managed by the Amherst Conservation Commission and located in a valley between Mack and Chestnut Hills in the northwest corner of the town, the 373-acre tract encompasses miles of wooded paths, clear flowing brooks, the Plumb and Harding Memorial forests, a beaver pond, and lots of birds, wildflowers, and elbow room for those weary of crowds and concrete. The short loop hike outlined here takes you to a beaver pond, with an excursion to Lookout Rock, a large granite outcrop.

Joe English Reservation is bounded on two sides by the 2,800 acre United States government satellite tracking station in New Boston, which is a well-managed wildlife preserve in itself but closed to the public. In the 1940s and 1950s the area was used as a practice bombing range. Joe English Hill is located on the tracking station property about three miles north of Joe English Reservation.

Joe English was a real person, a Pennacook Indian named Merrimacomet. "Joe English" was the derisive name given to him by members of his tribe in Massachusetts who banished him to New Hampshire for befriending the white settlers. According to legend, Joe was hunting one morning and was surprised by a small group of Indians who were intent on capturing him. The braves chased Joe up the slope of the hill that now bears his name, confident he would not escape the rocky precipice that awaited him on the other side. Joe, who was known for being a swift runner, managed to escape by finding shelter under an overhanging rock. From his hideaway he watched his pursuers crash through the underbrush and tumble to their deaths over the steep rocks.

Joe English Reservation is home to a wealth of wildflowers. In the springtime you'll find bluets, meadow rue, hepatica, false hellebore, violets, lady slipper, trailing arbutus, dwarf ginseng, and jack-in-the-pulpit blooming along the banks of the brooks, roadsides, and grassy areas. The springtime is an ideal time to search for woodland wildflowers which peak in late April and early May. Sunlight is able to pass through the branches of the hardwoods before the leaves emerge, warming the soil and providing energy from nutrients in the soil. Later, when the leaves shut out the sunlight, these woodland plants go quietly to sleep.

You may have noticed that many spring wildflowers are white. That's because they have been formed underground the previous year and no pigment has been developed. When the temperature becomes favorable, many of these flowers rise up into the light and air and take on various hues, among them blue, red or yellow. A pamphlet entitled *Wildflowers of the Joe English Conservation Area* details the flowers you'll find here and the month they first appear. The guide reminds you that many wildflowers will not survive after being picked and moved from their natural woodland environment.

Southern New Hampshire Calendar for Wildflower Blooms:
April: Arbutus, blood root, hepatica, marsh marigold, purple violet, shad bush. *May:* Bunchberry, columbine, flowering dogwood, fringed polygala, wild ginger, hobble-bush, Lady Slipper, nodding trillium, painted trillium, jack-in-the-pulpit. *June:* Blue flag, bristley locust, June pink, mountain laurel, pitcher plant.

April is also a good month to seek out vernal pools -- small woodland ponds that serve as breeding sites for wood frogs and salamanders. The wood frog survives the winter buried under leaf litter by producing a glycogen substance which allows up to 40 percent of its body to repeatedly freeze and thaw without causing damage to the cells. About 2.5 inches long with a dark mask below the eye, which leads into a distinctive white line along the upper lip, the wood frog lays its eggs in communal nests, with each spherical, jelly-covered egg clump containing about 1,500 eggs. Another spring visitor is the peeper whose high pitched, short call in chorus sounds like the ringing of sleigh bells. Though they are easy to hear, spring peepers are difficult to see because of their small size. If you ever come upon a thumb-nail-sized frog with a brown cross on its back, you've found one.

After a rainy day look for delicate purple, scarlet, and maroon capped mushrooms hiding among the tall ferns. Others look like tiny orange fingers hugging the ground, pure white sponges or are wineglass in shape. In June, mountain laurel with its showy large clusters of pink to white cup-shaped flowers bloom in profusion in the woods like mounds of snow.

Access: To get to the trailhead from the Manchester area, drive west on Route 101 to Horace Greeley Road (8 miles from the junction of 101 and 114). Continue on Horace Greeley Road for 0.5 mile. Turn left onto Brook Road. The parking area is 1.5 miles further at the end of the road.

Old stone wall, a common sight in the New Hampshire woods

Description: The blue-blazed trail starts southwest at a signboard (maps vailable) in the parking lot and enters a quiet forest of maple, beech, birch, and oak. Shortly afterwards, the path turns right to run along Hammond Brook which is worth a detour to see the brilliant red Cardinal flower (the only wild lobelia) sprouting from the dry stream bed in late summer. Lifting its flaming clusters of two-lipped scarlet flowers, this striking plant, one to three feet tall, seems to beg your attention. Cardinal flower is probably the most brilliantly colored wildflower.

After crossing a plank bridge, the trail continues to follow Hammond Brook. Dense thickets of moutain laurel flourish on both sides of the path. After crossing a trickle of a stream on a small plank bridge, the path brightens as the woods thin out to a brushy area dotted with stubby pines. In late summer goldenrod and wood aster grow here and the air is thick with the aroma of sweet fern.

Shortly afterwards, the path turns right (the blue trail continues straight to follow Hammond Brook). You'll cross a small brook and continue through a corridor of mountain laurel, then begin a gradual descent. Look here for violets, dewberry, and gold thread. The gold thread gets its name from the orange-colored creeping root stalks, by which it spreads. The plant has rich, glossy, green leaves somewhat like strawberry leaves, and the dainty white flowers rise from the basal leaves to a height of three or four inches in earliest summer.

Shortly you'll come to the yellow-blazed Eagle Trail junction on the left -- an interesting path that moves over hilly terrain past a Black Gum (tupelo) swamp. Tupelo is not commonly found in New England. The leaves of this medium-sized tree turn scarlet in the fall and its blue-black berry-like fruit is a favorite of many species of wildlife.

Soon after the Eagle Trail junction the trail widens as the footing changes to a dirt-gravel firmness. After walking past a low row of hemlocks that march off to the right, you'll come to a junction with Brook Road which was once a thoroughfare to the town of New Boston. Continue right on Brook Road for 50 yards. At this point the leaf matted, red-blazed trail to the beaver pond, a three minute walk, turns left into the woods.

At the pond, cross a wooden footbridge, then step over the rough paths that lead to the shoreline. Over the years the beavers have been in and out as inhabitants, leaving as the food supply dwindled and returning when it had replenished itself. The beavers have built a mud-and-stick dam spanning Joe English Brook. Growing along the edge of the pond are poke weed, Carolina yellow-eyed grass, loosestrifes, blueberry and hobble berry bushes, the whorled leaves and pink flowers of sheep laurel, and a sea of pickerel weed spikes the shallow water. You can stay for a while and keep an eye out for songbirds which include yellow warblers, nuthatches, and unobtrusive vireos whose persistent song give a better clue to its presence than its drab color and fidgety nature. From the distant woods you may hear the tapping of a hairy or downy woodpecker. Wood duck, Canada geese, and blue heron have also been known to visit the pond.

When you have finished communing with nature, continue on the red-blazed trail which heads into the woods beyond the footbridge. You'll cross Clean Brook, then shortly afterwards arrive at Lookout Rock where the view is mostly wooded. From Lookout Rock, the trail drops down a hill. Turn right to join the blue trail which soon turns right at another junction. Continue across Joe English Brook on a wooden footbridge to Brook Road. Turn right to retrace your route back to the parking lot.

Optional extensions: Joe English Reservation offers many more miles of hiking opportunities in addition to the ones outlined here. Another popular access is 0.8 mile up Chestnut Hill Road. There is a small parking area on the left with a map available. This section leads through the A. H. Plumb Memorial forest with good views northwest of Joe English Hill. Chestnut Hill Road is located off Horace Greeley Road about a mile beyond the Horace Greeley-Brook Road junction. The A.H. Plumb Memorial forest can also be accessed from Brook Road. The trailhead (blue-blazed) is located on the right side, 0.8 mile from Horace Greeley Road. Park in the school bus turn-around 0.1 mile below the trailhead on the left side of Brook Road.

Map for Hike 15

Purgatory Rd.

P

UPTON

×888

Purgatory Falls

East Ridge Trail

Middle Fall

Janet Trail

N

Contours in feet (20 foot intervals)

USGS: NEW BOSTON

| 0 | 1/2 | 1 MILE |
| 0 | 1000 FEET | 0 | 500 m | 1000 m |

Printed from TOPO! ©1998 Wildflower Productions (www.topo.com)

15

Purgatory Falls

Rating: Moderate woodland walk leading to a rugged gorge and waterfalls. The return trip follows an old bridle path through hardwood and spruce. *Caution:* The trail can be wet and slippery in places; the stream may be dry in late summer.
Distance: 2 miles
Hiking time: 1.5-to-2 hours
Lowest elevation: 430 feet
Highest elevation: 775 feet
USGS Map: New Boston
Other Maps: Mont Vernon Historical Society map

This hike will take you to a place called purgatory, but it is anything but an unpleasant experience. Straddling the Mont Vernon-Lyndeborough border and owned jointly by the towns, the 40-acre Purgatory Falls Conservation area is a tranquil oasis for those seeking solitude and a respite from the bustle of the everyday world. For years this was a meeting spot for families on weekend outings, church picnics, and Fourth of July celebrations. In the late nineteenth century, H.A. Hutchinson, the enterprising owner of the falls, parlayed the popularity of the site into a recreation area that included a viewing bridge, dancing pavilion, bowling alley, and bandstand. According to town histories, more than two thousand people attended a dedication ceremony in August of 1889. At one time a hermit lived here, who used to set his whiskers on fire and burn off his beard when it grew too long. Today, all that remains of "Hutchinson's Grove" are a few foundation stones and iron rods in the rocks that once supported bridges.

Purgatory Falls is an interesting place to visit in the early spring when huge slabs of ice sheath the steep, moss-covered rock walls rising from the basin floor. The water thunders through the chasm like a freight train, spouting over the lip of a 10-foot high cliff and into a wide rocky bowl.

Access: Take New Hampshire 31 North out of Wilton. One-half mile beyond the South Lyndeborough Village Store, turn right onto Center Road. Continue 5.4 miles to Johnson Corner Road on the left. Follow Johnson Corner Road for one mile to Purgatory Road. After 0.4 mile on Purgatory Road, it turns to a dirt surface. Continue another 0.8 mile to the Echo Valley Camping area. Keep to the right of the entrance sign and continue 0.1 mile. Park in a pullout to the right.

[*Note:* For access to Lower Purgatory Falls, see page 121.]

Description: From the parking area, the yellow-blazed trail descends immediately into a hemlock forest with a mix of beech, red oak, birch and maple. Shortly, the trail moves past the waters of Purgatory Brook to the left. After crossing a footbridge at 0.2 mile, you'll continue (right) on the Purgatory Brook Trail which stays close to the stream. Ten minutes from the start of the hike, you'll come to a ledgy area at the top of the Upper Falls. **Extreme caution** should be exercised here because there are no handrails or safety barriers. Here you can look down at the brook as it surges and dances through a deep flume before tumbling over the lip of a cliff into a frothy pool.

A large pothole known as the Devil's beanpot is located on the other side of the flume in the granite shelf beyond a string of iron posts in the rock that once supported bridges for viewing the falls. (You can get a view of the Devil's Beanpot on the return trip.) Legend has it that the devil once attempted to lure the townspeople of Mont Vernon to this lonely gulf by promising to cook them a baked bean supper

Purgatory Falls

with "all the fixings." At first, all went according to plan, but just as the Evil One reached out for the black cauldron of beans, the intense heat caused his foot to sink in the rock -- resulting in a string of expletives that frightened the people away.

From the ledgy area at the top of the falls, the trail continues to the left on the edge of the ravine, then swings down to the gorge. A sign points to a spur which leads to the bottom of the upper falls. Pick out a sun-warmed rock to loll on and feel the pulse and rumble of the waterfall as it plunges into the frothy basin. Take some time to watch the sunlight reflect off the water as it dances in firelight patterns on the curved rock face of the cliff rising steeply from the pool. You may even want to peel off your boots and socks and soothe your feet and weary spirit.

Purgatory Falls is full of devilish allusions. The rock bowl is sometimes called Hell's Kitchen. The Old Boy's Face (Giant's Head or The Indian Head) is a rock profile in a grotto on the basin floor. The pulpit, overhanging rock, and hog rock are other geological formations in the gulf that will keep your imagination active for a while.

There is a real feeling of isolation as you stare down at the seething waters and steep forested banks of the ravine. Jumbles of boulders deposited by the ancient glaciers and splayed tree roots clinging tenaciously to the steep banks like long deformed fingers only add to this eerie primordial aura. When you've finished admiring the natural beauty of the falls and exploring for geological features, continue on the trail.

The route swings slightly away from the gorge, onto higher ground in the woods, then moves past overlooks and back down to the stream past another cascade and a view of the rugged ledge cliffs rising on the opposite side of the brook. Minutes later, at 0.6 mile, you'll reach Middle Purgatory Falls which drop through a narrow crack in the rock. A steep 150-foot spur leads to the bottom. (A cave inside the rock wall here is known as the Devil's Den.) From Middle Purgatory Falls, the trail moves uphill and out of the gorge. At 0.7 mile, the trail passes a junction sign pointing to the East Ridge Trail.

The Devil's Beanpot

[*Option*: At this junction you can shorten the hike and take the East Ridge trail, which levels out after ten minutes and crosses a woods road before arriving back at the foot-bridge. A 5-minute walk brings you back to the parking area.]

The other option at this junction is to continue on with the described hike. From the East Ridge Trail junction, the Purgatory Brook Trail continues (right) downhill to a stone wall at 0.9 mile, follows the top of a glacial ridge next to the stream, then drops down to a bridge at 1.1 miles. After crossing the bridge, the trail follows an old carriage road for 200 feet, then bears right and uphill at a sign marking Janet's

Trail. [*Note:* At the time of this writing (late fall of 1999), there was a 1.5-mile trail in progress connecting the upper and lower falls systems.]

Janet's Trail returns on the west side of Purgatory Brook adjacent to high cliffs overlooking the gorge. The trail follows an old bridle path through hardwood up the ridge. After five minutes, it levels out somewhat and turns to the right. At 1.4 miles, the trail passes into a hemlock forest within earshot of the gurgling stream 250 feet below. At 1.6 miles, the trail leaves the bridle path and moves closer to the cliffs looking down into the amphitheater below the upper falls. 150 feet before the upper falls, a steep spur leads to the amphitheater, which is also called The Devil's Kitchen, and a view of the falls.

At 1.7 miles, Janet's Trail reaches the cliff area at the top of the upper falls. Here you can get a closer look at the Devil's Beanpot (not recommended for young children). Using caution, ease yourself down the outcrop of ledge to the rock shelf. An indentation at the edge of the pothole enables you to step inside. The pothole would certainly hold a lot of beans! After crawling back out, take a moment to check out the Devil's footprint (an imprint of a foot embedded in the rock next to the pothole). From the ledgy area at the top of the falls, the trail follows the stream back to the footbridge and returns to the parking lot at 2.0 miles.

Lower Purgatory Falls Access: From Johnson Corner-Center Road intersection, turn left onto Center Road. Continue for 3.1 miles (toward Milford) to North River Road (Fitch's Corner). Turn left onto Purgatory Road. The McClellan Trail sign is 0.5 mile further on the left.

The McClellan Trail wends 0.4 mile through a hemlock forest, then drops into the Purgatory Brook ravine. Short spurs from the trail lead to the bottom and top of the Lower

Purgatory Falls. The Lower Falls spread across a ledge and drop twenty feet into a pool. Surrounded by ferns and mountain laurel, the site is popular with photographers and artists because of the unusual natural lighting in the area. The trail continues up the stream past cascades and glacial boulders, then climbs out of the ravine and loops back on a carriage road to the Purgatory Road trailhead. Total distance is 1.5 miles.

Sightseeing: After your hike, you may want to drive a short distance to an excellent view of the Lyndeborough Mountains and Wapack Range. At the intersection of Johnson Corner-Center Road, turn left toward Milford and drive 0.5 mile to Pead Hill Road. Continue 0.6 mile for a spectacular view of the mountains across an orchard.

If you have time, you may want to visit Mont Vernon, a charming hilltop community that was once a popular summer resort that boasted several grand hotels, a golf course, and numerous boarding houses. The most imposing of these establishments was The Grand which was topped by a two-story cupola, where guests could watch the movement of ships in Boston Harbor through telescopes. With the advent of the railroad in the mid-1800s, Mont Vernon was a three-hour trip from Boston. The arrival of summer people tripled the normal size of Mont Vernon's population. Picnics at Purgatory Gorge no doubt received top billing. Beginning in the 1920s, however, the era of the grand hotel began to decline. One by one, the big hotels burned to the ground and all that remained were several buildings used as boarding houses.

You can still see the concrete steps of the Grand and two private residences that once were caretaker "cottages" on top of Prospect Hill. To get there from the center of the village, turn right onto Grand Hill Road (next to Deland Memorial Library) and continue right up Prospect Hill for 0.4 mile. The road continues as a loop around the site of the Grand.

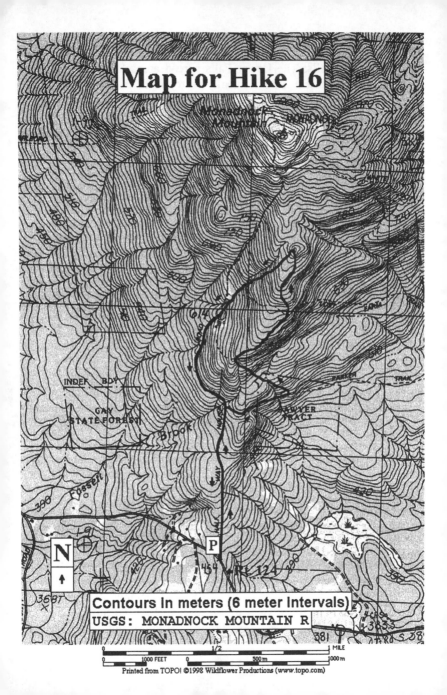

Map for Hike 16

Contours in meters (6 meter intervals)

USGS: MONADNOCK MOUNTAIN R

Printed from TOPO! ©1998 Wildflower Productions (*www.topo.com*)

16

Bald Rock - Mount Monadnock

Rating: Strenuous. The main section of the hike follows the Cliff Walk Trail, past several historical landmarks to a prominent hawk-viewing area. Challenging stretches of ledge will prove too strenuous for young children. An optional extension is a steep one-mile trail to the summit.
Distance: 3.6 miles (Optional extension 5.6 miles)
Hiking Time: 3.5 hours (Optional extension 5.5 hours)
Lowest elevation: 1,500 feet
Highest elevation: 2,640 feet (Optional extension 3,165 feet)
USGS Map: Monadnock
Other Maps: NH Division of Parks & Recreation Map, New England Cartographics Map, AMC Guidebook Map; SPNHF Monadnock-Sunapee Greenway Trail Guide

Praised in poems, the inspiration for countless paintings and photographs, Mount Monadnock has been a hiking mecca for thousands every year. The famous have found their way here - Thoreau climbed its peak on four separate occasions and Emerson called it an airy citadel. The second most climbed peak in the world (the first is Japan's Mount Fuji), Mount Monadnock has a network of forty miles of maintained trails, many of which lead to its 3,165-foot summit.

Most hikers take the popular White Cross or White Dot Trails, which begin near the warden's cabin just north of the Monadnock State Park Headquarters area, where there is year-round parking. A popular route is up the White Dot trail and down the White Cross trail (four miles round trip; hiking time 3-to-4 hours). The hike outlined here begins at another popular site, the Old Toll Road Trailhead (seasonal parking), and follows the Cliff Walk Trail to Bald Rock, a prominent outcrop and hawk-viewing area. The one-mile White Arrow Trail offers an optional hike to the summit. There is a $2.50 per person service charge; children under 12 are free. Make sure that you bring plenty of water, warm clothing for fall or spring hiking, and a sturdy pair of boots, but not your dogs.

Access: Take Route 101 West to Route 202 South in Peterborough. Continue to Jaffrey and follow Route 124 West for 5 miles. The Old Toll Road Parking Area is off Route 124, three miles beyond the main access to the Park.

Description: The hike begins at an elevation of 1,500 feet on the Old Toll Road near a booth and beyond the gate at the north end of a 65-car parking lot. Maps of the trails are available at the booth. Originally, the Old Toll Road carried guests up to the Halfway House Hotel. Over the years, a number of hotels were built on this site. The earliest one, the Grand Monadnock Hotel, was erected on the summit in 1823. Among the first guests was Ralph Waldo Emerson.

From the parking area, the road rises gradually through a mixed hardwood forest. In 15 minutes you'll reach the junction with yellow-blazed Parker Trail. Turn right onto the Parker Trail. The walking is easy now, but boulders lining the steeply-sloped woods to your left are an indication of the rugged ledge you will soon encounter. After ten minutes, you will turn onto the Cliff Walk Trail on the left. (The Parker Trail continues to State Park Headquarters.) The Cliff Walk Trail is well-marked by white C's painted on rocks; it follows long sections of ledge on the southeast side of the mountain. The trail rises immediately to a jumble of boulders and ledge. As you continue for the next ten minutes over these giant rocks, the going gets very rugged and can be slippery in places. The strenuous trail alternates through hardwood and spruce forest and ledge, with many good outlooks to the south and southeast.

The Cliff Walk Trail is well-marked by white C's painted on rocks

About one hour from the start of the hike, you reach the junction with the Point Surprise Trail on the left. Just before the Lost Farm Trail junction, you'll come to the first of several "seats" or lookouts. In this case, it's Ainsworth Seat, named for Jaffrey's "first settled minister." Two minutes ahead on the right, just beyond the Lost Farm Trail junction, lies Thoreau's Seat -- a long, smooth rock outcropping. The Thoreau Trail enters from the left here. Like the famous naturalist, you may want to stop and admire the view which stretches southeast to the Temple and Wapack Mountain ranges, with a checkerboard pattern of meadows, farms, and lakes dotting the Contoocook River Valley below.

Just ahead on the trail to the right is Emerson's Seat. Just beyond the Do Drop Trail junction on the left, you'll scale a steeply-sloped vertical ledge to emerge at a spectacular out-look. The Noble Trail enters to the left here. The craggy summit of Grand Monadnock looms to the north, while in the distance to the southwest lie Gap and Little Monadnock Mountains. A few minutes more on the trail brings you to the Wolf's Den on the left, a jumble of ledges and caves. Nearby is the "Graphite Mine," a vein that was worked about 1849. Flakes of graphite were collected here in barrels and rolled down a ramp to the Halfway House clearing.

A final section of flat ledge will require you to use hand and toe-holds. Five minutes of scrambling will put you on the Bald Rock Ledges. Bald Rock itself is a large schist outcrop. Just below is an interesting rock pedestal called the Pulpit. On the eastern part of the ledge is a cube-shaped erratic inscribed with the words "Kiasticuticus Peak." Years ago, Bald Rock was the only open spot on the mountain, for Mount Monad-nock was once covered to its summit with trees. The mountain's craggy shoulders and summit were eventually exposed by severe forest fires, some of them purposely set by early homesteaders to smoke out wolves threatening their sheep.

The summit of Mt. Monadnock from Bald Rock

From Bald Rock you can see Monadnock's southwestern false summit which is topped by a weathervane. Perhaps the most spectacular sight is the view of Monadnock's craggy summit rising from across the forested valley to the north. Bald Rock is used as a vantage point by the Audubon Society for its hawk counts because of the clear view it affords across the Contoocook River Valley. There is also less obscuring haze to look through here, compared with the view from the summit.

If you do see hawks, there is a good chance they will be broadwings, which are about the size of a crow, with broad, rounded wings and short tails that spread out like a fan. Broadwings usually stay close to the ridges where thermals, columns of warm air, are forced up the slopes. Using minimal effort, these hawks spiral to great heights, then tuck their wings and descend in a long, slow glide to catch the next thermal. Sunny September and October days are the best time for hawk-watching, especially after the passage of a cold front with the wind freshening from the northwest.

When you are ready to return, locate the Hedgehog Trail to the west, painted in white on the rocks, which leads to the old toll road. The steep, rocky path moves down a narrow opening to the left of Bald Rock, then enters a dark spruce woods. Look for a sign on a tree here. After ten minutes, you will use caution as the trail is full of rocks and roots, and the Hedgehog Trail joins the Sidefoot Trail on the left. Continue downhill on the Sidefoot Trail and you will emerge after a few minutes at a large clearing. This is the former site of a series of Halfway House Hotels. The first was built in 1860 and the last one burned in 1954. Look for an inscription on a rock face, denoting the site near the signs for Hello Rock, Point Surprise, and Thoreau Trail on the eastern side of the clearing. From the Halfway House clearing, follow the old Toll Road for the half-hour walk back to the parking lot.

Optional extension: If you have time, you can take the White Arrow Trail for one mile from the Halfway House clearing to the summit. Look for a sign at the northwest end of the clearing. Built in the eighteenth century and the oldest trail to the summit, the White Arrow Trail starts off steep and rocky, and continues that way to the top. In some places it is like walking up stairs, because in 1861 a geodetic survey team laid in about 400 stone steps to assist them in hauling their equipment to the top.

As you continue, you will notice unusual markings that look like turkey tracks or fossils on the slabs of schist. These are sillimanite crystals which stand out due to the weathered surface of the rocks. They were formed during a period of folding when intense heat and pressure within the rocks changed the mineral composition. Many of these crystals were changed into mica. Shale metamorphosed into schist and sandstone became quartz, which you can easily see in the white streaks in the rocks.

One half-hour from the Halfway House clearing you will emerge from the trees and suddenly see an open ledge looming above you that looks like it might be the summit. When you arrive, you will realize you are not at the top, but turn around and you can take in the spectacular view that unfolds to the south. The town of Troy, New Hampshire, Gap Mountain, Little Monadnock Mountain, the Wapack Range, and Mount Greylock are all visible. You can also see Bald Rock directly below you. From this high point, the path climbs and you will scramble over the rock outcrop for the final 30-minute ascent to the top, where you can observe Mount Monadnock's famous view of the six New England states.

On a fair day the view embraces an area 150 miles in diameter, and some 200 lakes and ponds may be seen. One hundred miles to the northeast, you can see the peaks of the Presidential Range, especially when they are snow-capped, with Mount Washington in their midst. On an exceptionally clear day, you can see the ocean and Boston's Prudential and John Hancock buildings. Mount Tom and Mount Greylock in western Massachusetts are discernible, as well as the long line of Vermont's Green Mountains to the west.

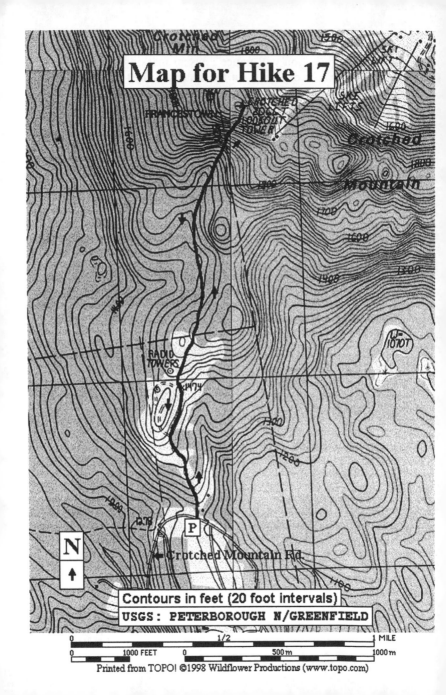

Map for Hike 17

Crotched Mtn

FRANCESTOWN

CROTCHED
DOG
LOOKOUT
TOWER

Crotched
Mountain

RADIO
TOWERS

1474

1010T

P

← Crotched Mountain Rd.

N

Contours in feet (20 foot intervals)
USGS: PETERBOROUGH N/GREENFIELD

0   1/2   1 MILE
0   1000 FEET   0   500 m   1000 m

Printed from TOPO! ©1998 Wildflower Productions (www.topo.com)

17

Crotched Mountain

Rating: A moderate hike that begins on an old service road and continues through abandoned pastures and spruce woods to a promontory with an outstanding view of the Contoocook River Valley to the west.
Distance: 3.6 miles
Hiking Time: 2.5 hours
Lowest Elevation: 1,300 feet
Highest Elevation: 2,066 feet
USGS Map: Peterborough North, Greenfield

Rising like a fortress from the south-central upland, Crotched Mountain offers sweeping views of Mount Monadnock and the Contoocook River Valley from its 2,066-foot summit. In the late 1800s, and for many years afterward, Crotched Mountain was home to a thriving blueberry enterprise. Local shopkeepers employed entire families to pick the fruit. The freshly picked berries were shipped in crates to the Boston market by train. Depending on your schedule, you may elect to pick a bucketful for yourself. They are small, deep blue, and sweeter than the high bush variety.

Access: To get to the trailhead from the Manchester area, take Route 114 West to Route 13 South in Goffstown. Follow Route 13 for seven miles to New Boston, then travel Route 136 West for 12 miles to Greenfield. From Greenfield take Route 31 North for 0.9 mile. A large white sign saying

"Crotched Mountain Rehabilitation Center" directs you to the right onto Crotched Mountain Road. Continue uphill for 1.5 miles until you see the main entrance sign for the Crotched Mountain Rehabilitation Center. Drive 0.2 mile farther and park off the right shoulder opposite the trailhead gate.

Description: The Greenfield Trail begins heading north, just beyond a metal gate and a sign: *Active driveway--Do not park here*. The trail starts out on a gravel road that immediately forks left as it climbs uphill. In late summer the air is heavy with the scent of sweet fern, sometimes called "small boy's tobacco," that grows in the shady and sterile soil alongside the road here. Young oak, birch, and maple dominate the south-facing slope, along with quaking aspen whose fine-toothed, rounded leaves are anchored by flattened stalks, causing them to tremble in the slightest breeze. The quaking aspen's leaves are shiny green and pale below; in the fall they turn clear golden. In August blackberry brambles intertwine with abandoned stone walls in the woods to the left of the trail here.

Five minutes of walking brings you to a clearing where three-sided shelters owned by the Crotched Mountain Rehabilitation Center sit off to the right. Continue uphill. At a semicircle of large boulders, the road comes to a fork. The short walk up the gravel road to the left leads to a ridge and hawk-viewing area with good views of Mount Monadnock to the west. Bear right at this fork. As you start up the road, one of the three summits of Crotched Mountain shows itself briefly above the trees. Crotched is a three-peaked mountain with heights in Francestown, Bennington, and Greenfield. After five minutes you'll reach a small cairn. At this point you'll leave the gravel road and continue to the right on a grassy path where wild blueberries grow on both sides of the trail on the exposed ridge in late summer.

Crotched Mountain

The trail continues on the grassy path, with boulders beginning to mix into the footing, then turns left and northeast. The trail descends into a cool spruce woods, and then slender maple and birch trees stretch overhead. After walking past an unusually shaped boulder on the right and a spur trail on the left, you'll reach a small stream that may be dry in late summer. The trail turns uphill again as you step through a gap in a stone wall and thread your way through waist-high juniper. At this point you may feel like you're walking in a trench.

Shortly, a large granite outcrop, Lookout Rock, provides a rest spot with a view of Mount Monadnock (somewhat obstructed by trees) to the west. Always a grand sight, the old mountain is especially impressive in late afternoon when sparkles of light color its broad shoulders. From Lookout Rock, a five-minute uphill climb brings you to a junction with the Bennington Trail on the left, near a stone wall. A small sign points the way to the summit. From here, the top is only 10 minutes away, but take your time as weblike tree roots and boulders can make this the most difficult stretch of the hike. Just before the summit, a double blaze on a spruce tree directs you west to a scenic view. Be sure to take it. The scenic view site consists of a series of bed-sized boulders that provide the perfect setting for lunch. The view is obstructed by trees, so make your way down the sloping rock wall to a lower promontory. Before you do this, take note of your surroundings so you won't have trouble finding the trail when you return.

Once you emerge from the trees, the broad valley spreads before you in a patchwork of lakes, steepled churches, and ribbon roads. The buildings comprising the Crotched Mountain Rehabilitation Center nestle on a lower ridge to the south with North and South Pack Monadnock Mountains and the rest of the Wapack Range marching off behind. In the foreground to the right of the Crotched Mountain Center lie Greenfield State Park and Otter Lake. Mount Monadnock anchors the horizon to the southwest. In the foreground the broad waters of Powder Mill Pond, part of the Contoocook River, expand into what looks like the body of a goose and its beak. Powder Mill dam crosses the "beak." The prominent mountains rising beyond Powder Mill Pond are Skatutakee and Thumb Mountains in Hancock. Farther in the foreground close to the base of Crotched Mountain is Lake Whittemore.

To the right of Powder Mill Pond lies the town of Bennington, and if you continue your gaze in that direction you can see a gray plume of smoke rising from the smokestack of the Monadnock Paper Mill in Bennington. Antrim with its white steepled churches sprawls in the valley three miles farther north, with Bald Mountain anchoring the ridge on the western edge of the town to the south. Stratton Mountain ski area in Vermont is visible on the western horizon.

Sightseeing: Nearby is Greenfield State Park, with 400 acres located on the shores of Otter Lake. It offers swimming, fishing, camping, 250 tent sites, restrooms, showers. Contact Greenfield State Park, Box 203, Greenfield NH   03047. Phone 603-547-3497.

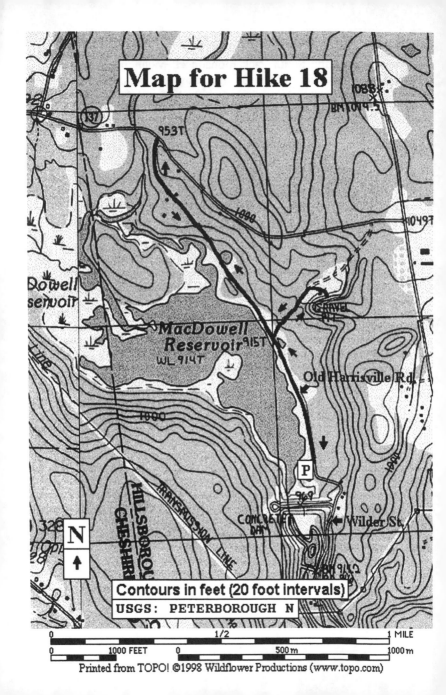

Map for Hike 18

953T

1088

BM1014.2

137

1000

10497

GRAVEL PIT

Dowell
servoir

MacDowell
Reservoir 915T

WL 914T

Old Harrisville Rd.

1000

P

969

CONCRETE DAM

Wilder St.

HILLSBORO
CHESHIRE

TRANSMISSION LINE

BM 916

N
↑

Contours in feet (20 foot intervals)

USGS: PETERBOROUGH N

0 _____ 1/2 _____ 1 MILE
0 ___ 1000 FEET ___ 0 ___ 500 m ___ 1000 m

Printed from TOPO! ©1998 Wildflower Productions (www.topo.com)

18

Edward MacDowell Lake

Rating: An easy stroll along the shore of a reservoir with views of waterfowl and wildflowers.
Distance: 2.2 miles
Hiking time: 2 hours
Lake Elevation: 912 feet
USGS Map: Peterborough, Marlborough
Other Maps: U.S. Army Corps of Engineers map

The Edward MacDowell dam on Nubanusit Brook in Peterborough was built between 1948 and 1950 by the Army Corps of Engineers as part of a network of flood control projects in the Merrimack River basin. 1,100 feet long, 25 feet wide, and 67 feet high, the massive dam and flood control reservoir protects Peterborough, Hancock, Bennington, and other small towns in New Hampshire and Massachusetts by holding back flood waters from the major tributaries of the Merrimack River.

Over 1000 acres of land and water have been leased to the New Hampshire Department of Fish and Game as part of the corps project philosophy to promote the use of land and water while conserving the natural environment. The Department provides opportunities here for outdoor recreation including picnicking, boating, fishing, hunting, cross-country skiing, and hiking. The 2.2-mile round trip Wetland Wander Trail hike outlined here follows gravel Old Harrisville Road along the eastern shore of Lake MacDowell, and offers good opportunities to see wildflowers and waterfowl.

Edward MacDowell Dam

Access: From the intersection of Routes 101 and 202 in Peterborough, continue on Route 101 for 2.2 miles to the sign for Edward MacDowell Lake. Turn right onto Union Street. Go 0.6 mile to Wilder Street (left) and continue uphill. After 0.4 mile you'll come to the main building and visitor information board. Continue driving beyond the entrance gate downhill for 1000 feet, to a picnic shelter. Park in the lot opposite a yellow gate.

Description: Your hike starts on the Old Harrisville road that runs along the eastern shore of MacDowell Lake. The biggest draw of this short walk is the opportunity to observe the abundance of bird life in the wetlands lining the road: woodducks, mallards, mergansers, ring necked ducks, and Canada geese. Herons stalk through the marsh grass of these waters, there are osprey, and occasionally, reports of an eagle sighting. The vast network of marsh at the isolated north end of the lake make this a popular nesting area and regular stopover for a variety of waterfowl during their spring and fall migrations. To the west, beyond the rock studded shoreline across the lake, moose, fisher, deer, mink, coyote, fox, and an occasional bear make their homes in the mixed forest. Soon after you start out, a good view of the Skatutakee Mountain Range shows itself to the north. As you continue, the "Pinnacle" in Dublin pokes into view to the northwest.

In June look for blue eyed grass and clouds of bluets blooming along the road, and yellow (bullhead) pond lilies bobbing on the lake surface. The smallest of pasture wildflowers, bluets have a delicate pale blue bloom and usually form large clusters in early spring. Local names for this ubiquitous vernal flower are innocence, Quaker ladies, nuns, and blue-eyed babies. Pickerelweed shows in abundance along the banks of the weedy lake. You will also find arrowhead here. The white flowers of this appropriately named plant begin to appear in July and may be found in

141

bloom through August and September. Sometimes called Duck or Swamp Potato because of the potato-like tubers produced along its submerged root system, arrowhead is a favorite with ducks and geese who fed on the starchy tubers. You'll also find goldenrod, steeplebush (hardhack), Joe Pye Weed, and meadowsweet. Steeplebush is easy to recognize because of its wine-purple color. Meadowsweet is found over much of the same area as hardhack but its leaves are a little broader and its color usually white. Buttonbush also grows here, identified by its ball-like flower and seed clusters which open up to fuzz as they ripen. The fruits have some appeal to Mallard ducks.

At 0.5 mile you'll come to a "beach" area on the left and you will see another road that spurs off to the right. This is the Dune Lookout Trail which leads to a sand pit area with good views of Crotched Mountain and Mount Monadnock. Take a few minutes to walk up the road. After 0.2 mile you'll reach a large sand dune. A path to the right of the mound leads to the top where you'll get a good view of Crotched Mountain to the northeast and Mount Monadnock to the west. After this brief detour, return to the Harrisville Road and "beach" area. Take some time to sit and look out at Goose Island across the water to the left.

Continue on old Harrisville Road (Wetland Wander Trail) which becomes more wooded on the right. At 0.6 mile you'll come to a yellow gate. It is closed, but step around it to continue your walk. A road to the left leads to a new boat ramp and parking area. MacDowell Lake is an ideal body of water for canoes and johnboats with trolling motors. Canoeists and kayakers will find orange buoys marking the channel of Stanley Brook. The lake is shallow, 3 feet deep on average, and ideal for fishing for hornpout, bass, pickerel, and perch. Beyond the gate, there is marsh on both sides of the road and it provides an ideal habitat for mallards to build their nests. Goldfinches, swamp sparrows, eastern kingbirds, owls, and piliated, downy and hairy woodpeckers are other birds to observe. There is a chance you'll see a red-winged blackbird lighting atop a cattail or bulrush, or hear his "konk-a-ree" call. If you look closely to the left and northwest, a small waterfall is visible at the upper end of the lake.

At 0.8 mile you'll reach another yellow gate, and 0.1 mile beyond this gate you'll reach Richardson Road (gravel). (0.2 mile further is Spring Road, an East-West road that leads to Route 137.) At Richardson Road, turn around to retrace your steps back to the picnic shelter. After you've finished hiking Old Harrisville Road, you'll want to walk across the 1,100-foot-long dam. Follow a set of concrete steps down the 67-foot high rock slope embankment to check out a marker on the gatehouse wall indicating the record high water level (949.8 feet mean sea level). The record was established during the 1987 April flood when a combination of melting snow and heavy rainfall filled the lake to 126% of its capacity. April of 1987 was the only period in the history of the dam when the water crested the spillway.

The 100-foot-wide spillway is located 3.2 miles upstream (northeast) of the dam at Halfmoon Pond in Hancock, and it empties into Ferguson Brook which in turn flows into the Contoocook River. The overflow system on the dam works on the same idea as an old-style bathtub, where a drain near the top of the tub allows safe drainage and prevents water spilling over the sides if you've left the water running. Three one-foot-thick steel gates that run down to the water level regulate the flow of the lake. The gatehouse channels water downstream through a concrete conduit which stretches several hundred feet under the dam. MacDowell Lake drains an area of 44 square miles -- from the eastern slopes of Mount Monadnock in Jaffrey to Lake Nubanusit in Hancock -- and the reservoir has a capacity to store 4.2 billion gallons of water. Five different lakes run into the reservoir. Prior to the creation of the system of reservoirs and local protection works, cities and towns in the Merrimack Valley basin experienced frequent and sometimes devastating floods. Especially eventful was the Flood of 1936 and Hurricane of 1938. The Hurricane of 1938 alone caused 750 million dollars in damage and led to the creation of much of the Corps' flood control projects.

Complete your walk to the west side of the dam where you'll find a circular parking area, restrooms, and picnic tables on park-like fields of grass. To the right of the restrooms, a 10-minute loop through the woods on the Log Boom Trail leads back to the dam site. The two-mile, yellow-blazed West Ridge Trail leads off the Log Boom Trail to Route 137. By following Route 137 and the Spring, Richardson, and old Harrisville Roads, it is possible to complete a 4.5-mile circuit around the lake.

MacDowell Dam is open 8 a.m. to 8 p.m. during the recreational season (Memorial Day-Labor Day), and 8 a.m. to 3 p.m. the rest of the year. Tours of the dam and gatehouse are given periodically during the summer recreation season, along with interpretative programs on wetlands and forest management techniques. Information is available at the project office where you can pick up maps and brochures and view charts and aerial photographs of the dam.

Sightseeing: The town of Peterborough is worth a visit before or after your hike. A handsome town of dignified homes on hilly streets with a large number of red brick buildings in the Georgian Revival style that are a favorite with photographers, Peterborough was the model for Thornton Wilder's "Our Town." The Town House, a monumental structure built in 1918, serves as the center for town meetings as well as cultural events. It is a copy of Faneuil Hall in Boston. The Georgian Revival style building underwent a restoration in 1995.

A commercial and cultural center for the Monadnock region, Peterborough is also the home of the famed MacDowell Colony and Peterborough Players Summer Theater. The Peterborough Town Library was founded in 1833 and was the first free public library in the U.S. to be supported by taxation.

In the 1800s, Peterborough was a prosperous manufacturing community with a half dozen mills. The Phoenix Cotton Factory was the principal plant and it employed hundreds of people for well over 100 years until its demise in 1922. A tailrace below the mill ran in a wide stream in the lot below the Town House on its way to the Contoocook River and carried water from the great mill wheel to supply power for a number of other activities which included a planing mill, shoe factory, and basket shop. For years the canal was called the "Little Jordan" because the Mormon and Baptist churches used the stream for baptisms.

Two old mill buildings have been moved from the banks of the Nubanusit River onto land owned by the Peterborough Historical Society and are the focus for its educational programs. There is an historical and genealogical library, exhibits, and museum open year round: Monday through Friday, 10 a.m. to 4 p.m.; July & August during weekends from 1 p.m. - 4 p.m.

Map for Hike 19

P
Monadnock St.
Old Mill Rd.
Brook
COUNTY ROAD
369T

P
← Upper Gap Mountain Rd.

Contours in meters (6 meter intervals)
USGS: MONADNOCK MOUNTAIN L

N
↑

0   1/2   1 MILE
0   1000 FEET   0   500 m   1000 m

Printed from TOPO! ©1998 Wildflower Productions (www.topo.com)

19

Gap Mountain

Rating: An easy hike following a section of the Metacomet-Monadnock Trail through abandoned pastures, and offering rewarding vistas along the way and a stunning view of Mount Monadnock from the summit of Gap.
Hiking Time: 1 hour
Distance: 2 miles
Hiking time: 1.5 hours
Lowest Elevation: 1,378 feet
Highest Elevation: 1,862 feet
USGS Map: Monadnock
Other Maps: New Hampshire State Parks Trail Map, AMC Metacomet-Monadnock Trail Guide

Comprising three low peaks and named for a gap between its southern and middle summits, Gap Mountain beckons the hiker to its serenity and lush surroundings. Except for one rocky stretch, the one-mile trail to Gap's middle and northern peaks is minimally demanding. There is an optional access, a northern approach (see page 150).

Access: The trail to Gap can be reached off Route 12 in Troy, 1.5 miles south of the town common. Look for Gap Mountain Road just beyond the highway's town line marker for Troy-Fitzwilliam, opposite Bowkersville Road. After 0.8 mile, staying on the tar road, you'll come to Upper Gap Mountain Road. A sign will direct you to the "J.Tyler" place. Continue (left) for 0.2 mile and park off the shoulder near the wetland.

View of Mt. Monadnock from Gap Mountain

A short walk up the paved road will bring you to the white colonial Tyler place and grassy woods road beyond the garage. Follow the woods road beyond a green metal gate for 100 yards until you reach a large white pine tree near a break in a stone wall on your right and to the east. The Metacomet-Monadnock Trail begins near a brown Gap Mountain -- Monadnock State Park information kiosk. There is a white blaze on a rock to the right.

Description: The white-blazed trail starts off steeply through typical New Hampshire woodland growth of birch, beech, oak, maple, and white pine. You will come immediately upon the remains of a shed on your right. The trail is at first flanked by waist-high juniper, but before long you'll reach a meadow populated by old apple trees. Gap was once open pasture and a valuable summer grazing area for cattle brought up from farms in northern Massachusetts.

Beyond the abandoned pasture, the trail becomes deeply rutted, followed by the most difficult section of the hike. Before maneuvering up this stretch, look to the right for a trail that leads to Gap Mountain's 1,862-foot south peak, a 15-minute walk. After taking this side trail, return to the main trail and maneuver up a series of flat, sloping, vertical rocks that may require hand and toeholds. You will then see the view opening up. Gap's 1,862-foot south peak is clearly visible, as well as a great view of Troy to the west. The south peak is a SPNHF-owned natural area known as the John Noble Memorial Reservation.

A few steps beyond this outlook brings you to the middle summit and a striking view of Mount Monadnock to the northeast. Just west of Grand Monadnock lies Bigalow Hill, an elongated hill shaped by the erosional force of ice moving southeast during the last Ice Age. The glacial ice bulldozed up the north slope of the hill, polishing the rock, then slid down the south side, creating crags and steep cliffs. This polishing and grinding action carved out a hill shaped like a breaking wave, which geologists call a sheepback. The ice also produced drumlins, which are rounded little hills composed of boulder-filled clay called till. Drumlins were created when the till that the ice was dragging along got caught on protruding knobs of bedrock. The whole area that is east, southeast, and south of Mount Monadnock is populated with drumlins down to the border of Massachusetts.

The view to the south-southwest is of Little Monadnock Mountain, Rockwood and Bowker ponds, and the church spires of Fitzwilliam. An excellent view of the entire 21-mile-long Wapack Range can be seen to the east. To the west you can see the town of Troy, sprawled out in the valley against a backdrop of distant Vermont peaks, several of which are scarred by ski trails. Troy is the home of Troy Mills, the third oldest mill in the United States. In the nineteenth century, the mill was famous for producing horse blankets. Today the complex produces carpeting products for cars.

From the middle peak, the Metacomet-Monadnock Trail continues northeast to Gap's north peak. With just a few minutes' walk, you descend the ledge area, walk past a boggy meadow and then a stone wall. Return by the same route.

Optional Access: From the intersection of Gap Mountain Road and Route 12, drive 1.3 miles north to Troy. Turn right onto Monadnock Street, passing Troy Mills, and continue 2.5 miles to Old Mill Road on the right. Old Mill Road is 0.3 mile beyond the Inn at East Hill Farm. Park near the sign that reads: Bridge closed. Walk up the dirt road marked with blue blazes, going past a waterfall. After 10 minutes, the trail enters the woods and continues into a field. Look for a brown wooden sign in the field: "Gap Mountain -- Mount Monadnock Park." Follow blue blazes into the woods. Look for a gap in a stone wall and step through it. Continue following blue blazes over a footbridge. At an intersection near a fallen tree, the hike continues as part of the white-blazed Metacomet-Monadnock Trail to North Peak of Gap Mountain.

Atop Gap Mountain, with Mount Monadnock in the background
Photo by Joanne Adamowicz

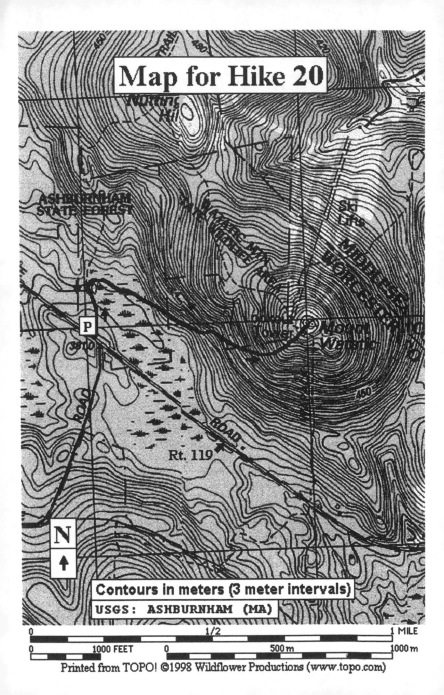

Map for Hike 20

ASHBURNHAM STATE FOREST

Notting Hill

SKI Lift

P

Tower

Rt. 119

ROAD

N

Contours in meters (3 meter intervals)

USGS: ASHBURNHAM (MA)

0   1/2   1 MILE

0   1000 FEET   0   500 m   1000 m

Printed from TOPO! ©1998 Wildflower Productions (www.topo.com)

20

Mount Watatic

Rating: A moderate climb through a hemlock forest to open ledges and outstanding view of the mountains to the north and the Boston skyline on the horizon to the southeast.
Distance: 2.4 miles
Hiking time: 2 hours
Lowest Elevation: 1,200 feet
Highest Elevation: 1,832 feet
USGS Map: Ashburnham (Massachusetts)
Other Maps: Wapack Trail Guide and Map; Midstate Trail Guide

Rising in Ashburnham, Massachusetts and marking the beginning of the 21-mile-long Wapack Trail, Mount Watatic makes the perfect outing for new or experienced hikers.

Access: To reach the trailhead from the Manchester area, take Route 101 West to Route 31 South in Wilton. Continue for 13 miles to the junction with Massachusetts Route 119. Travel west on Route 119 for 1.5 miles to the small town of Ashby, Massachusetts. Continue for 5 miles more and look for a small parking area to the right (north), enclosed by a chain linked fence. The Wapack Trail starts at the north end of the parking lot on an old cart path beyond a metal gate.

Description: The Wapack Trail is blazed with yellow triangles and begins heading north in conjunction with the Midstate Trail, "The Way of the Indians, " a 91-mile-long Massachusetts footpath that begins at the Rhode Island border and terminates on Mount Watatic. For more information about the Midstate trail, call 978-874-5626 or 978-874-2445.

This Mt. Watatic fire tower is no longer standing

Shortly you'll cross a brook that flows through a culvert under the road, and then move past a small pond to the right. After a brief rocky upgrade and 0.2 mile, the Wapack and Midstate trails turn right and east into the woods for the one-mile journey to the summit. A signboard with a map detailing the entire route of the Wapack Trail can be viewed here. (The blue-blazed State Line Trail continues 0.9 mile north to the Massachusetts/New Hampshire border. After crossing Mount Watatic, the Midstate Trail briefly follows Nutting Hill Road before merging with the State Line Trail which then continues on to the New Hampshire/Massachusetts state line.)

Continuing on the hike, for the first few minutes you will pass tall white pines, hardwoods sporting odd-shaped burls, and an enormous split boulder. For the next ten minutes you'll climb steadily uphill through a quiet hemlock forest, over boulders and tree roots, before coming to a fine view of Mount Monadnock to the northwest. The trail continues along a stone wall and leads to a ledge area where scaly flecks of mica shimmer in the sunlight. Little Watatic Mountain rises to the southwest; to the south is 2,006-foot Wachusett Mountain, the highest point in Massachusetts east of the Berkshires. The trail now turns left. After stepping through an opening in a stone wall, you'll move uphill and south through another grove of hemlock. Shortly you'll reach a wooden shelter (in poor condition). A two-minute walk from the shelter brings you to the summit. Turn right to walk out to the open ledges.

The view from the top is spectacular, especially to the north where the entire Wapack Range unfolds before you in a sea of green bumps. The early settlers used Watatic as a resort for observation in their travels from the seacoast to the Connecticut River. The view to the northeast of the Wapack Range includes the Lyndeborough Mountains, Joe English Hill, and the Uncanoonucs in Goffstown, New Hampshire.

Further east lie Saddleback Mountain and the Pawtuckaway Mountains marching toward the New Hampshire coast. Further to the northeast you can see the blue silhouettes of the Belknaps near Lake Winnipesaukee, and on a clear day, the White Mountains are visible. Mount Monadnock is clearly distinguishable to the northwest, with Stratton Mountain further to the west in Vermont. A labyrinth of lakes with Indian names glisten like jewels behind you to the southwest. To the west-southwest, Mount Greylock is visible in the far corner of Massachusetts.

From the main summit make your way down to Watatic's lower, eastern summit 450 feet away. From there you'll get a good view southeast to the buildings of the Boston skyline. After enjoying the views and lunch on the open ledge, you may want to search the summit rocks for the geodetic marker, initials and dates of those who have passed this way before you. Retrace your steps to return to your vehicle.

Sightseeing: After you complete your hike, you may want to explore Ashby Center on Route 119. Perched above the town common is the First Parish Church which was built in 1809 as a meetinghouse and church. The octagonal steeple holds a 1280-pound church bell cast at the Paul Revere Foundry in Boston. A clock keeper who is appointed on an annual basis by the town climbs the rickety stairs every week and winds the clock with a handcrank. The position of Town Clock Winder came into being in 1846 when Louis Gould presented the "Howard" clock made by the Stephenson, Howard and Davis Company of Boston to the town. The gift came with the stipulation that the clock always be maintained at the expense of the town of Ashby. (The church owns the building and bell tower; the clock and bell belong to the townspeople.) There is a view from the tower that includes the Boston skyline off to the east; Mount Watatic to the west, and the fields and forests of New Hampshire to the north.

Behind the church in the old burial ground you'll find the small gravestone of Prince Estabrook, a black soldier who fought at Lexington and Concord. Estabrook is believed to be one of the soldiers in the rowboat in Emanuel Leutze's famous painting *Washington Crossing the Delaware*. To the west of the church is a Revolutionary-era home which was once the Wyman Tavern. Inside there is an unusual dance floor that moves independently of the building as the boards were formed and bent to act as a springboard.

View from Mt. Watatic

Map for Hike 21

Goose Pond

WL 193T

P

Gravel Pits

Pump Sta

Surrey East Rd.

N

Contours in meters (6 meter intervals)

USGS: KEENE R

| 0 | 1/2 | 1 MILE |

| 0 | 1000 FEET | 0 | 500 m | 1000 m |

Printed from TOPO! ©1998 Wildflower Productions (www.topo.com)

21

Goose Pond

Rating: An easy loop around a wilderness pond with an opportunity to see a variety of birds, animals, and plant habitats along the way.
Distance: 1.3 miles
Hiking time: 1 hour
Pond elevation: 635 feet
USGS Map: Keene
Other Maps: City of Keene map

A wilderness area in Keene? Three miles north of the shops on Main Street, you'll find the 500-acre Goose Pond preserve and recreation area. Through careful purchase and negotiated protection of land, the city has assured that the quiet coves, islands, inlets and surrounding wooded hills of this vast tract will remain a refuge for wildlife and source of enjoyment for future hikers, nature lovers, and bird watchers. A popular place for the citizenry of Keene to relax after a day at work, the walk around Goose Pond takes about an hour to complete, although numerous diversions will tempt you to extend that time. Along the way you'll see a variety of birds and water-fowl, and you may even get a glimpse of a deer, fox, raccoon, fisher, beaver, or mink who make their homes in the wooded hills surrounding the pond. In addition to hiking, Goose Pond offers many opportunities to birdwatch, picnic, snowshoe, or cross-country ski in season. Hunting, swimming, and motorized vehicles are prohibited. Overnight camping and fires are allowed by special permit.

Goose Pond

Access: From the Manchester area, take Route 101 West to the Main Street exit in Keene. Continue to the head of the square, go halfway around the rotary, and turn onto Court Street. Follow Court Street for 2.1 miles to Surry East Road. The parking area is 0.9 mile farther.

Description: The white-blazed trail begins to the left of the parking area and quickly moves uphill past huge white pines with an understory of hemlock. In minutes you'll descend into a clearing of meadow-sweet, brambles, and stubby pine before entering the woods again where a white arrow on a rock points the way upward.

A stone wall continues to follow you on the left, and polypody fern blankets the forest floor. Soon you'll get your first glimpse of Goose Pond off to the right through the lower branches of oaks and maples. Slender white birch trees bend gracefully toward the open water and highbush blueberry bushes border the perimeter of the pond. Turn left to follow the path northeast along the shoreline. As you walk, look for piliated woodpeckers who use the rotting stumps and decaying trees in the open beech and oak forest for their feeding ground. A large, wary bird with a gray body with patches of white and a brilliant red crest, the piliated woodpecker flies with an irregular flap of its wings and has a distinctive cry, a loud, nasal *kuk-kuk*.

In a few minutes you'll walk under an arbor of feathery hemlock grown so thick with boughs that little sunlight reaches the ground. Shortly you'll approach the first of many hidden coves and inlets. Mallards rest here in the sheltered waters in the fall and your sudden appearance may startle them into a frenzied flight as they whip the water with a flurry of wings. Canada geese, black ducks, buffleheads, and mergansers can also be seen here. The trail continues across Rainaford Brook, the first of three watercourses you'll cross, then circles along the shore of a cove where there are half submerged trees with stubble branches and upturned root stumps. You'll continue through another grove of hemlock and beech trees. For an interesting view of the shoreline, follow the small trail that leads to the tip of a peninsula.

Return to the main trail to continue along the shoreline of another cove where you're likely to see more ducks floating peacefully on the calm waters near a small island. Shortly you'll step through a gap in a stone wall. Look for an arrow on a tree that directs you (right) toward the shoreline. Use caution here as it is easy to go left instead. Whenever you're in doubt, stay in sight of water. After crossing Anacoluthic

Brook and moving through another open beech forest, a side trail leads (right) to another peninsula where there is a huge boulder and good view of a small island across a dark narrow channel of water.

Tall white pines and hemlock hug the shoreline as the trail moves past a hillside outcropping of ledge that has become a natural rock garden of wintergreen. You'll step on more stones to cross Reliance Rivulet which dances down from the hillside to the left to enter the pond. In the fall there is an especially nice view southwest of the distant hills across the pond. From this point the walking becomes more difficult as the trail narrows and tree roots grow underfoot. After passing a boulder-studded cove, the path moves away from the shoreline to enter a cool hemlock woods.

Several minutes later you'll come to an earthen dam where a large sawed-off stump provides a good resting spot to sit for a while and enjoy the cooling breezes. The trail reenters the woods and widens. After 100 yards, look for a trail marker painted on a tree. Be careful here. It is very easy to follow the trail left which leads to dirt roads that head out toward the park boundary and city access road. Instead, continue right and toward the pond, past a boggy area where sphagnum moss jiggles on the water along the pond's edge and stumps poke through the water.

By now you've undoubtedly noticed that Goose Pond is actually more like a lake in size (42 acres). Over 100 years ago the townspeople of Keene built two dams to double the surface area of the pond (a good part of the newly flooded area was formerly bog and forest). The impetus for the enlargement was the concern expressed by the citizenry after the Great Fire of October 19, 1865 which destroyed a good portion of Central Square and exhausted the water supply of the town wells. The dams were built to enlarge Goose Pond and bring new water to Keene, and in November 1868 a pipeline of hollowed-out logs channeled water to the city's new fire hydrants. Although Goose Pond has not been used as a public water supply for many years, it remained a potential source for Keene until 1984. That year the city designated the 500-acre area a wilderness park, never again to be used as a water supply.

After you walk past the boggy area, the trail continues along the shoreline through more massive hemlock and pine. Numerous shoreline outlooks provide especially good views of wooded hills to the northeast. Shortly you'll come to a large cove, then step through a gap in a stone wall to emerge from the hemlock woods at a grassy clearing. Continue walking across a square block concrete dam and overflow spillway (the outlet flows into the Ashuelot River). 100 yards beyond the spillway your hike ends at the path on the left that leads back to the parking lot.

Pickerel weed

Map for Hike 22

Hurricane Rd.

P

Hyland lookout Hyland

460T lat

Hyland lo.

HYLAND HILL
LOOKOUT STATION

N
↑

Contours in meters (6 meter intervals)

USGS: KEENE L

0   1/2   1 MILE

0   1000 FEET   0   500 m   1000 m

Printed from TOPO! ©1998 Wildflower Productions (www.topo.com)

22

Hyland Hill

Rating: Moderate. A short but steep walk up a jeep road that leads to a ninety-foot tower and outstanding view of the city of Keene and the Ashuelot River Valley.
Distance: 2.5 miles
Hiking time: 1.5 hours
Lowest Elevation: 984 feet
Highest Elevation: 1,509 feet
USGS Map: Keene

A half hour walk on a jeep access road brings you to one of the most eyepopping vistas in the Monadnock region, with Keene nestled below the craggy summit of Mount Monadnock to the east, and Mount Greylock, Ascutney, and other lofty peaks vying for your attention from all points of the compass.

Access: To get to the trailhead from the Manchester area, take Route 101 West to the Route 9 exit in Keene. Continue for 0.5 mile to the West Street exit. Turn left at the stop sign and continue 0.6 mile to a flashing yellow light. Turn left onto Arch Street and drive past Keene High School and Alumni Field. At 0.2 mile beyond Alumni Field turn right onto Hurricane Road. Continue 3.8 miles and look for an unmarked dirt road. The road turns sharply downhill and into the parking area. If the road is muddy, park at a small pullout to the left which has room for several cars.

Description: The trail starts steeply northwest on a rocky jeep road. Immediately, you see a small brook trickling down the hillside in a grove of hemlock lining the road to the left. New England aster, ferns, goldenrod, and jewel weed grow on both sides of the road here. As you continue through a mixed hardwood forest, intersecting logging roads spur off in all directions. Many of these roads are trails used by mountain bikers whom you're likely to meet on the way up. Twenty minutes of steady walking brings you to a crest in the road where the trail comes to a fork and levels out about 3/4 mile up. You will notice a change in the gradient immediately. Stay to the left (the mountain bikers exit to the right).

You'll continue over a flat section for 0.2 mile before the road turns ledgy and steepens again (the direction is south). After stepping through an opening between two green iron rails, a final five-minute ascent past a corridor of hemlock brings you to the 1,509-foot summit and 90-foot tower. The tower is perfectly safe, but you will hear and feel the rattle of the wind whistling through the supports, handrails, and antennae as you ascend the stairs. The Hyland Tower is a link in a network of lookout stations in southern New Hampshire (Pitcher Mountain in Stoddard, Croyden, Mount Kearsarge in Warner, and Federal Hill in Milford) and Mount Grace in Warwick, Massachusetts. When a puff of smoke is detected, it is crossed with observers at those stations to pinpoint the exact location of a fire. Visitors are welcomed by the watchman who will identify various peaks and mountains when he is not busy scanning the horizon for smoke.

The 360-degree view reaches into Massachusetts and Vermont. On a clear day to the southwest you can see the top of Mount Greylock. Almost due south is Meetinghouse Hill in Winchester; further beyond is Mount Grace State Forest in Warwick, Massachusetts. Mount Monadnock sits on the horizon to the southeast, with the city of Keene in the valley below. The sprawling body of water to the southwest is Spofford Lake, one of the largest bodies of water in the Monadnock region, and you can see Mount Wantastiquet in Hinsdale and Chesterfield. To the northeast in New Hampshire, the ridge of Sunapee and the top of Cardigan Mountain in Orange are both visible on a clear day. To the north you can see Fall Mountain in Walpole and Langdon and small sections of the Connecticut River to the northwest. In the spring when there is still snow on the ski trails, seven Vermont ski mountains are quite prominent: Mount Snow, Stratton, Haystack, Bromley, Magic, Timberridge, Killington. The highest point you can see north is Mount Ascutney.

Mountain bikers on the trail

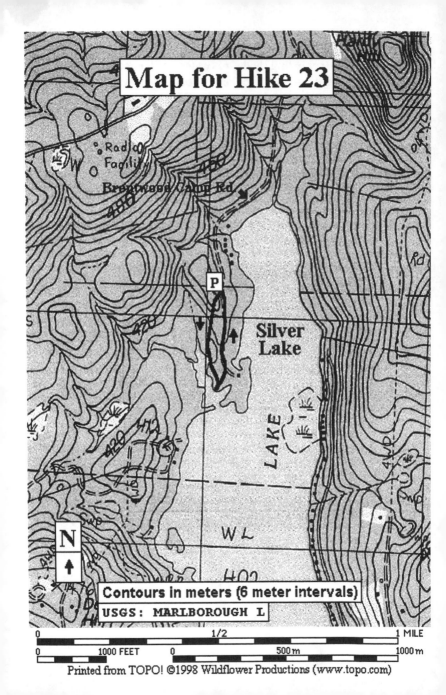

Map for Hike 23

Radio Facility

Brentwood Camp Rd

P

Silver Lake

LAKE

WL

N

Contours in meters (6 meter intervals)
USGS: MARLBOROUGH L

0	1/2	1 MILE

0	1000 FEET

0	500 m	1000 m

Printed from TOPO! ©1998 Wildflower Productions (www.topo.com)

23

Sucker Brook Cove - Silver Lake

Rating: An easy woodland walk that leads to a boulder perch and outstanding view of Mount Monadnock across Silver Lake.
Distance: 3/4 mile
Hiking Time: 45 minutes
Pond Elevation: 1,319 feet
USGS Map: Marlborough

Mount Monadnock is a spectacular sight from any direction, but especially when viewed rising above a lake. You can take in this sight by walking on an easy woodland trail to a boulder perch at the Audubon Society of New Hampshire Sucker Brook Cove Sanctuary at Silver Lake in Nelson.

Access: To get to the trailhead from the Manchester area, take Route 101 West to Dublin. Just beyond the red buildings of Yankee Publishing, the white steepled Community Church, and the Dublin Fire Department, turn right onto New Harrisville Road and continue eight miles to Nelson Center. Go south on Leadmine Road (between the old brick school house and the library). After 0.3 mile, just beyond a cemetery, bear right. Continue 0.6 mile to Brentwood Camp Road (left). There is a sign with the Sanctuary loon profile logo here. Continue 0.9 mile past camp buildings and look for a brown Audubon sign *Sucker Brook Cove Preserve Audubon Society of New Hampshire* and small parking area.

Description: Beginning at the parking area, the trail is blazed with yellow rectangles and leads uphill and south through a mixed forest of birch, beech, and hemlock with an understory of hobblebush. Bristly club mosses push up from the matted duff of the forest floor. In summer, one inhabitant of the moist woodland is the parasitic, fleshy white Indian pipe, sometimes called corpse plant or ghost flower; it grows four-to-eight inches tall with nodding flowers. Soon you'll come to a yellow-red trail junction. Continue left on the yellow trail downhill past gigantic boulders and into a grove of hemlock. Minutes later you'll get your first glimpse of Silver Lake through a tangle of alder bushes. As you skirt the shoreline, the twittering of birds reminds you that this is a wildlife habitat and you are here as a guest of nature. A decaying log ruffled in fungi, clintonia, shamrock-shaped wood sorrel, and wild sarsaparilla are things to be on the lookout for as you continue on the woodland path.

After five minutes the trail comes to another yellow-red junction. The yellow trail on the left leads to the road back to the parking area, so turn right to follow the red path for a short distance to a cove with a spectacular view of Mount Monadnock. The shoreline boulders provide an excellent vantage spot to sit and enjoy Monadnock and the sights and quiet sounds of the lake: the waves gently lapping the shore; swallows skimming across the surface of the water in search of insects; bumblebees working the bell shaped flowers of blueberry bushes that grow on the rocky shoreline along with Mountain Holly. Mergansers and loons also inhabit this lake, and you may see a mallard. The female mallard is a drab light brown whereas the male has an iridescent blue-green head, white neck band, and rust colored breast. The underside of the male is white and his wings are a dark, smoky color compared to the mottled down feathers of the female. Both the male and the female sport a speculum on their wings -- a triangular-shaped patch of bright blue with a border of white.

Sightseeing: Before or after your hike, you may want to visit the nearby towns of Nelson and Harrisville. Nelson is a handsome village laid out in 1752 and named for British naval hero Admiral Horatio Nelson. It has a beautiful town common, an old brick school house, and town hall reconstructed from an old meetinghouse (1787) which is also used as a contradance hall. Take a peek inside to see the knotted spruce floors exhibiting the ripples of time. There's also the one-room Olivia Rodham Memorial library, named for a nationally known botanist (1845-1920), and a Greek-and-Gothic Revival Congregational Church with a two stage bell tower.

Along the way to Nelson. you may want to stop at Harrisville, one of the most beautiful mill villages in New England. With its native brick buildings reflecting in the water of Nubanusit Pond, Harrisville is a favorite subject for photographers and painters.

Sucker Brook Cove

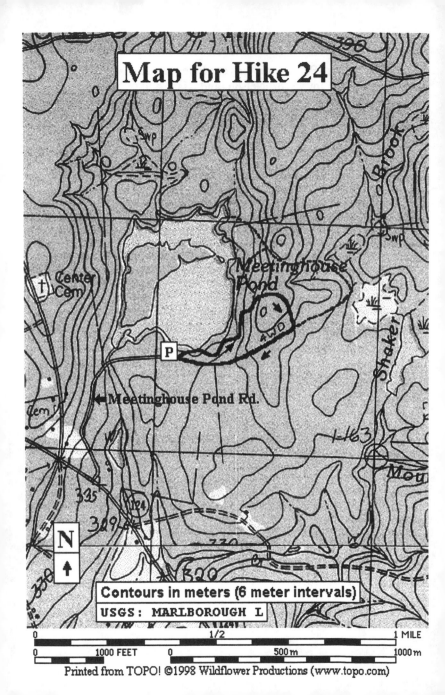

Map for Hike 24

Meetinghouse Pond

Center Cem

P

←Meetinghouse Pond Rd.

N
↑

Contours in meters (6 meter intervals)
USGS: MARLBOROUGH L

0   1/2   1 MILE
0   1000 FEET   0   500 m   1000 m

Printed from TOPO! ©1998 Wildflower Productions (www.topo.com)

24

Meetinghouse Pond

Rating: A pleasant woodland walk along the edge of a pond with numerous side trails leading to shoreline vistas. An optional route leads over a ridge and down to a beaver pond with opportunities to see signs of wildlife along the way.
Distance: 1 mile (1.5 miles optional Rocky Ridge trail)
Hiking Time: 1 hour (1.5 hours optional)
Pond Elevation: 1096 feet
USGS Map: Marlborough
Other Maps: Audubon Society of New Hampshire Field Guide Map

This is a pleasant woodland walk through mature stands of hemlock and pine along the edge of a 45-acre pond, Kensan Devan Sanctuary, on the western slope of Mount Monadnock. The one-mile route outlined here explores a rich variety of flora and fauna, and colorful mushrooms sprouting from the moist woods in late summer and fall.

Access: From the Manchester area, take Route 101 West to the Route 124 junction in Marlborough. Turn south on Route 124 and continue for 2.3 miles to the dirt Meetinghouse Pond Road. (**not** Meetinghouse Road). Continue 0.5 mile farther to the parking area and boat landing.

Optional Access: For a more scenic route to the trailhead in the autumn, take Route 101 West to Route 137 to Jaffrey. From Jaffrey take Route 124 West past lowlands ringed with fiery red maples, colorful hills, roadside yellow ferns, and purple asters. There are great views of the stony crown and broad flanks of Mount Monadnock on Route 124.

Description: The Winterberry Trail starts at the parking lot and boat landing. Look for a yellow metal rectangle nailed to a big red oak tree and the sign with the Audubon Sanctuary loon profile, along with a mailbox containing a trailhead register to record your observations. Before you begin your hike, you may want to take a short walk down to the pond to get a peek at the white and yellow water lilies and the water-loving plants growing on the shoreline, including sweetgale, high bush blueberry, maleberry, and mountain holly.

Mushrooms abound in late summer and early fall

As you start on the trail, you'll immediately enter a quiet hemlock forest grove where an abundance of mushrooms sprouts in late summer and early fall. You'll want to stop and admire the variety of shapes, sizes and colors before you move on. A rainy August day is an especially good time to look for mushrooms because during the late summer the humidity level of the ground is high. You will likely find milky caps -- a large, white capped common mushroom that tends to stain brown in age and has a cottony in-rolled margin. *Lactarius deceptivus* ("deceptive milky") is so called because if you score the gills, a milky excretion emits forth. Young milky caps are flat topped with button hole centers and edges that fold over. As it grows older, the cap of this mushroom uplifts like a funnel and resembles a goblet.

Another species you'll find here is the in-rolled-pax, a brown, pancake-like mushroom with a thick stalk and gills that stain reddish-brown. There are also purple capped mushrooms, yellow disk waxy caps, and the destroying angel, a pure white mushroom that grows beneath hemlock and belongs to the *Amanita* genus. Perfect white mushrooms are often poisonous. *Amanita* are responsible for 95% of all mushroom poisonings. Mushrooms can be very toxic. The Audubon field guide strongly recommends that you *never* consider eating a mushroom from the wild unless you really know what it is.

Despite their reputation, mushrooms do have a positive function. They work to decompose leaves and animal remains and they release antibiotics. There would not be any forests if it were not for fungi that reduce dead timber and forest litter to essential humus in the woodland floor. Mushrooms lack leafy green and are unable to manufacture starch, sugar, or other elements and must absorb them from dead wood or leaves, or soils enriched by plant remains. As mushrooms absorb from the stumps and old logs, the wood softens and falls apart. If you live in the Monadnock Region and are interested in learning more about mushrooms, you can join Monadnock Mushroomers Unlimited, an organization of amateur mycologists who study mushrooms in their natural habitat. Contact Monadnock Mushroomers Unlimited, P.O. Box 6296, Keene, N.H. 03431. You can also subscribe to the publication *Mushroom -- The Journal* by writing Mushroom, Box 3156, Moscow, Idaho 83843.

When you've finished with your mycology study, continue on the trail past ground cover of trillium, clintonia, bunchberry, and an impressive display of hobblebush with large, heart-shaped leaves at their base that turn bronze-red and purplish-pink in the fall. The shady shoreline of Meetinghouse Pond provides the ideal habitat for this viburnum, also called moosewood, which grows in dense thickets throughout the woods. Shortly you'll approach a side trail (watch for the blue dot on a tree) that leads to the pond and boulder studded cove. This is the first of several side trails leading to pond vistas.

As the main yellow-blazed trail swings away from the pond and uphill along the side of a ridge, the footing becomes rocky. More hemlock enshrouds you as you step over a bed of moss covered boulders; a large one to the right of the trail with a cluster of polypod fern clinging to its top. It is especially peaceful here. The trail turns left, back toward the pond, then moves through a gap in the stone wall. You'll notice a distinct change in the footing and forest community as the drier soil supports a greater hardwood population including maple, birch, white pine, and red oak. At this point you'll come to a junction (red-yellow). The yellow trail continues straight ahead as the Rocky Ridge Trail (see *Option* next page). Turn right on the red trail to continue on the Winterberry Trail which moves to higher ground to follow a logging road. After five minutes you'll come to an intersection with the Underwood Road. Turn right to follow Underwood for the final 10 minute walk back to the parking lot.

Optional extension: From the junction of red-yellow trails, follow the Rocky Ridge Trail for a few hundred yards, where a newly blazed red trail, Lee's Trail, turns left as you near the top of the ridge to lead down to the northeast end of the pond. This is a 10-minute walk to a nice view of the bog mat as you look back over the pond and south toward the parking lot. Chances are that you'll see Canada geese, wood ducks, and other waterfowl here, and your presence may flush out a few mallards as they noisily take to the air from the thick mat of lily pads choking the cove.

If you have more time, you can take the 1.5-mile yellow-blazed Rocky Ridge Trail, which will take you straight along the edge of the pond, then over a stony ridge and down to a beaver pond. Along the way you will have the opportunity to see numerous signs, tracks, and trails of wildlife. From the beaver pond, the trail continues to join the Underwood Road. Follow this back to the boat landing.

Sightseeing: Before or after your hike, you can explore Jaffrey Center, located 1.9 miles west of the town of Jaffrey. Here you'll find the handsome First Church (Congregational), and at the top of the green the Old Meetinghouse (1775), built to serve both as town hall and church. According to the *History of Jaffrey*, the huge granite doorstone of the First Church was drawn from Marlborough over Mount Monadnock by 14 oxen. The frame of the Old Meetinghouse was raised on June 17, 1775, the day of the Battle of Bunker Hill, and according to tradition, workmen could hear the sound of the distant cannons. Services were discontinued in 1844, and the building is now owned by the town of Jaffrey and used as a community house. The famed Amos Fortune lectures are held here.

Amos Fortune was a Black slave (born about 1710), who at age 60 purchased his and his wife's freedom. In 1781 he came to Jaffrey where he established a tannery, gaining respect for his honest work and earning a reputation as an upstanding citizen. At his death he left a fund to the town of Jaffrey, and today the bequest is used for educational purposes. The Amos Fortune Forum presents nationally known speakers in a series of free lectures held at the Meetinghouse on Friday evenings during July and August. The Meetinghouse is also used for Monadnock Music concerts. Next to the Meetinghouse you'll find the Little Red School House, maintained by the Jaffrey Historical Society. It is open Saturday and Sunday 2-4 p.m. in July and August.

Amos Fortune's gravesite is located in the old burying ground behind the Meetinghouse. His gravestone records that he "lived reputably and died hopefully." Also here are the gravestones of Willa Cather, the famous novelist who spent many summers in Jaffrey, and Hannah Davis, a Jaffrey resident who made, trademarked and sold the first wooden bandboxes used for women's bonnets in the United States. The Meetinghouse Cemetery is a peaceful place to visit with the craggy summit of Mount Monadnock serving as a backdrop. Near the First Church and Meetinghouse is Thorndike Pond Road which leads to an outstanding view of Mount Monadnock from the eastern shore across the water of Thorndike Pond.

Meetinghouse Pond

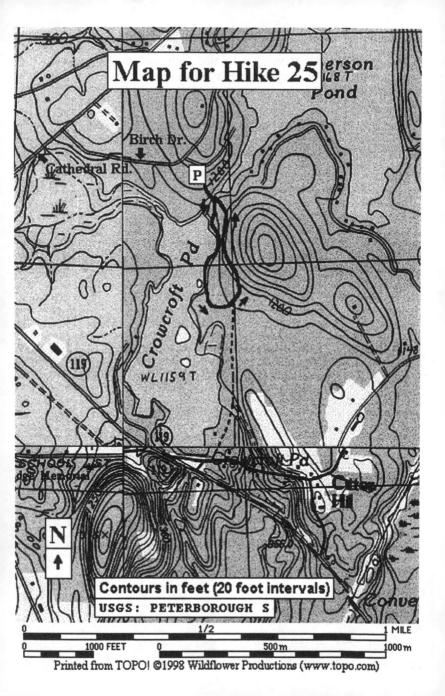

Map for Hike 25

erson
Pond

Birch Dr.

Cathedral Rd.

P

Crowcroft Pd

WL 1159 T

119

119

N ↑

Contours in feet (20 foot intervals)

USGS: PETERBOROUGH S

| 0 | 1/2 | 1 MILE |

| 0 | 1000 FEET | 0 | 500 m | 1000 m |

Printed from TOPO! ©1998 Wildflower Productions (www.topo.com)

25

Betsy Fosket Sanctuary

Rating: Easy. A short walk along the edge of a pond past hemlock and tall white pines, with an opportunity to see a variety of birds, wildflowers and wildlife.
Distance: 0.6 mile
Hiking time: 45 minutes
Pond elevation: 1,170 feet
USGS Map: Peterborough South
Other Maps: Audubon Society of New Hampshire field guide map

The trailhead for the Betsy Fosket Sanctuary of the Audubon Society of New Hampshire is located at the end of Emerson Lane -- a residential area of contemporary homes, manicured lawns and driveways. It is an unlikely start for a nature hike, and at first you may feel you are going out for a neighborhood stroll. But soon after crossing a stone bridge and entering the woods, all vestiges of civilization are quickly left behind. There are hemlocks, tall white pines, and stonewalls here, a pond, birds, and wildflowers. If you're lucky you may spy an otter, mink, or red fox, or discover bottled gentians that hide away in lush growths along the trail in August.

Access: The 35-acre, heavily wooded Betsy Foskct Wildlife Sanctuary is located at the northeast corner of Crowcroft Pond in Rindge, New Hampshire. From the junction of Routes 202 and 119 in Rindge, go east 1.5 miles on Route 119, then left on Cathedral Road. After 0.5 mile, at the Cathedral Estates sign, turn right onto Birch Drive. Continue 0.3 mile and turn right on Emerson Lane. Park in a cul-de-sac at 0.1 mile.

Crowcroft Pond

Description: After crossing a stone bridge, look for the yellow rectangle-blazed "Betsy's Trail" just beyond the brown Audubon Society of New Hampshire sign and mailbox where you can pick up a trail guide. Large, old-growth hemlock immediately curtains you off from the outside world and there is a palpable sense of peace and quiet. After briefly moving downhill and following the small stream that flows from Emerson Pond, you'll step through a gap in a stone wall and come to Crowcroft Pond.

The old dam at the outlet of Emerson Pond dates back to the late 18th century and has been in ruins for many years. Crowcroft Pond came into being when the water of Emerson Pond was diverted through a meadow. In the summer, pickerel weed with its spiky carpet of blue flowers and white water lilies choke the coves and fringes of the pond. Pickerel weed, common most everywhere in the shallow waters of ponds, is likely to take possession if given the opportunity. Only the cattail seems able to hold its own against it. There is a good view to the southwest of the pond here. In the distance you may spy canoeists paddling in and out of the quiet coves along the shoreline. Crowcroft Pond is privately owned. Canoeing is allowed, but restricted to the northern third of the pond.

For the next several minutes the trail continues along the shoreline, crossing stone walls several times and winding through groves of hemlock. Chipmunks scurry underfoot and along stonewalls; red squirrels chatter their warning and scold you from their treetop perches. Look for evidence of pillowing and cradling here -- mounds and depressions in the forest floor that is a sign of storm damage to trees. This wavy ground topography occurs when a tree is blown over and its root system is ripped from the ground. After the tree decays, a "pillow" or mound of dirt adhering to the woody parts of the upward root system is left in place, and a depression or "cradle" remains in the area where it was uplifted.

As you continue, sphagnum moss grows along the edge of the water and the forest floor is rich in a variety of groundcovers: clintonia, bunchberry, wild sarsaparilla, wood sorrel, star flower, wild lily-of-the-valley and partridgeberry (twinberry) - the small, round, evergreen leaves are always in pairs, and there are two blossoms. Shortly you'll reach a woods road. Turn right. The trail briefly follows the road, then turns left into the woods to parallel it.

A short time later you'll re-enter the woods to the right, step through another gap in a stone wall, and continue along the shoreline where you are apt to get a glimpse of a painted turtle sunning itself on a half-submerged log. The trail turns left back into the woods, then moves toward the shoreline again where you'll see a small pine tree-topped island that is a popular place with the birds. Red-breasted Nuthatches, hairy woodpeckers, and black-capped chickadees are some of the species found here.

The route continues on an easy walking surface of pine needles to a connector trail on the right which is blazed in red and leads to an outlook beyond a stone wall on the shoreline. Betsy's Trail turns left and rejoins the woods road. At this point you can turn right (south) to follow the road for 10 minutes to a wood plank footbridge and the dam site which creates Crowcroft Pond. The Audubon Society does not own this property, so be respectful of the property owner. If you turn left instead, the trail follows the woods road back to complete the loop to the parking area.

On moist, late summer days, you can see a variety of fungi sprouting from the forest floor, including Indian pipe, a small perennial plant often found in dark hemlock forest because it does not use sunlight to make its food, extracting it from fungi instead. The Audubon Trail Guide notes that bottled gentians grow along the trail from August through October. The gentian is easy to recognize but hard to find. The leaves come in pairs on opposite sides of the lower section of the stem but are whorled near the top. Looking very much like little narrow blue barrels pinched off at each end, the clusters of 1-to-2-inch blue flowers must be sought out in their own special haunt -- the moist ground of wet roadside banks.

Sightseeing: If you have time after you complete your hike, you may want to visit the Cathedral of the Pines -- a simple stone altar, bell tower, and wooden bench outdoor memorial to the American War dead, with Mount Monadnock providing a spectacular backdrop. Open 9 a.m. - 5 p.m., May to January. To get there, return to Cathedral Road and continue north for one mile. Further up the road is Annett State Park, picnic sites, and walking trails, with a 1/2-mile trail leading to Black Reservoir within 1,336 acres of woodland. Annett State Park is one mile north of the Cathedral of the Pines.

Another point of interest is located in Rindge Center, the 1796 Rindge Meetinghouse, one of the largest buildings of this type in northern New England, and one of the few remaining meeting houses still used as both town building and church. To get there, return to the blinking yellow light on Route 119 and drive 0.5 mile up Payson Hill Road.

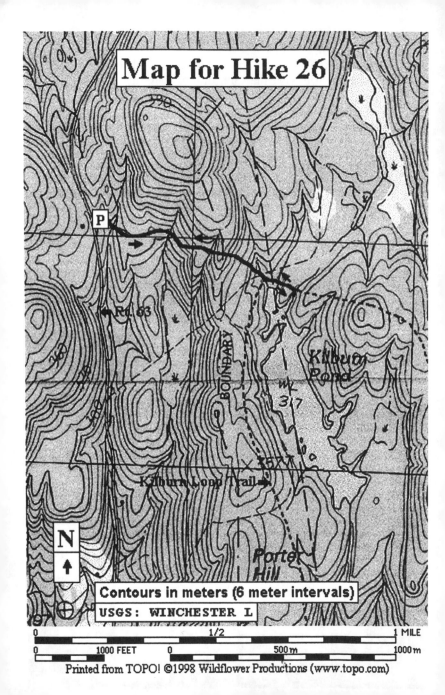

Map for Hike 26

P

Rt. 63

BOUNDARY

Kilburn
Pond

317

357

Kilburn Loop Trail

Porter
Hill

N

Contours in meters (6 meter intervals)

USGS: WINCHESTER L

| 0 | 1/2 | 1 MILE |

| 0 | 1000 FEET | 0 | 500 m | 1000 m |

Printed from TOPO! ©1998 Wildflower Productions (www.topo.com)

26

Kilburn Pond

Rating: An easy, forested walk to a 37-acre pond in New Hampshire's largest state park with an opportunity to see lots of migrating birds along the way
Distance: 1.5 miles
Hiking time: 1 hour
Pond Elevation: 1030 feet
USGS Map: Winchester
Other maps: Road and trails map, Pisgah State Park

Pisgah State Park is the largest property in the New Hampshire state park system and the second largest state park in New England. Located in the southwestern corner of New Hampshire along the Connecticut River, there are six trailheads leading into 13,500 acres of rugged wilderness, highland ridges, ponds, streams, wetlands, and old-growth pine and hemlock. At one time much of this land was privately owned and logging was an eminent industry. Today the only clues to this logging past can be found in the old skid roads and ramps, mill sites, cellar holes, and abandoned settlements that dot the landscape. With 50 miles of trails, outdoor enthusiasts have ample opportunities for hiking, bird-watching, mountain biking, cross-country skiing, picnicking, and fishing,.

Access: From Keene, follow NH 9 West to NH 63. Turn left and continue one mile to the town of Chesterfield. The Kilburn Pond trailhead is 3.5 miles farther on the left. Park in the newly built lot and begin your walk on Kilburn Road.

Kilburn Pond

Description: The gravel road immediately leads you east, past beech, birch, maple and oaks -- a riot of yellows, reds and oranges by early October. The fruit (mast) of the beech trees makes for good eating as each small prickly burr contains two or three small, triangular nuts which are highly prized by wildlife -- bear, deer, and many birds including wild turkey and wood duck. Beechnuts have a rich, delicate flavor that offsets the disadvantages (small size and difficulty of opening their thin but leathery shells). Another distinctive feature of this hardy tree is its smooth bark which hugs the trunk and branches of the trees even in old age. A smoky, dark tone is frequently noticeable on one side of the trunk, with still darker cracked areas around the base.

The trail descends immediately into a grove of hemlocks, then begins a gradual ascent. Tall, white pines are rooted firmly among ledge and chaotic jumbles of glacially scattered boulders in the woods. You'll continue through thickets of mountain laurel. The shiny leaves of this hardy shrub remain green throughout the winter, long after its showy pink to white flowers have died. Look for an interesting cleft boulder on the side of the trail to the left. A triangular-shaped hole in the large rock makes an ideal hideaway for chipmunks and other small critters. The path darkens again as you move through another grove of hemlock and approach the first real uphill section of the hike. Awaiting you at the top of the rise are slabs of granite, matted with rock tripe lichen. Rock tripe (genus umbilicara) resembles a leathery dark lettuce leaf of up to three inches wide, attached to a rocky surface. The trail levels out, swings left and right, then begins a descent.

In five minutes you'll connect with the Kilburn Loop Trail which continues to the right and south, a five-mile hike that returns east of the pond. A blue marked ski trail, the return loop for the Kilburn trail, leads to the left. Take a minute to walk down to Kilburn Pond past an impressive display of hobble bush. Sedges, rushes, blueberry bushes, and sphagnum moss grow along the edge of the water, and tall white pine and hemlock ring the shoreline. In early summer look for yellow bullhead lilies and squadrons of water bugs. Children will enjoy the gyrations of the speedy water striders and whirligigs (also called lucky bugs, submarine chasers, and write-my-names). The crimson-tailed dragonflies put on their own impressive aerial show.

Return to the ski trail and Kilburn loop junction where you continue to the left. You pass two marshy areas studded with standing and downed snags, and a red-and-white Winchester-Hinsdale sign, before reaching a pine needle softened path on the right that leads through the woods to a boulder outlook on the pond. Here you'll get an excellent view across the water and enjoy the warm southern exposure of the afternoon sun. Follow side paths to the left to get a view of the entire pond. Sit for a while and listen to the resonant clucking of chipmunks and other quiet forest noises. When you are ready to return retrace your route to the parking area.

Sightseeing: Another nearby hike is the Ann Stokes Loop Trail, located in the 488-acre Madame Sherri Forest on the eastern slope of Wantastiquet Mountain in Chesterfield. This 2.5-mile loop starts at the "castle" ruins of Madame Sherri's former summer home and goes around the 20-acre Indian Pond. From the Kilburn Pond trailhead, drive 2.9 miles on NH 63 toward the village of Chesterfield. Turn left onto Stage Road. Continue 0.2 mile and take a left onto Castle Road, drive another 0.8 mile and bear left onto Gulf Road. Drive 1.8 miles to a red SPNHF gate marking the Madame Sherri Forest.

Madame Sherri castle

You can also explore the nearby village of Ashuelot and Winchester after you finish your hike. From the trailhead, drive south on Route 63 for 4 miles to Hinsdale and turn left onto Route 119 East. Continue past old brick mills and houses crowding the narrow riverbank and hills of the forested valley. From the mid-to-late 1800s, the Ashuelot River was active from a manufacturing standpoint, boasting numerous textile and paper mills. The wooden container industry in Winchester at one time employed hundreds of people who produced kegs, buckets, pails, and barrels; at one point the New England Box Company ran six stationary sawmills and as many as 53 portable sawmills -- the largest mill was located on Round Pond in Pisgah State Park.

In the hamlet of Ashuelot, 3.5 miles from the junction of Routes 63/119, you can walk on the 169-foot two-span Upper Village Ashuelot Covered Bridge. Built in 1864, it is a town lattice truss type bridge with a pedestrian walkway. Or visit the Thayer Public Library (Hours: Tuesday and Thursday from 1 to 8), which is housed in a white colonial home that was a tenement house for the workers of the Sheridan Woolen Mill in the late 1800s.

Winchester lies 2.5 miles east of Ashuelot. Here you will find the former Winchester National Bank and old Winchester Memorial Church, both Greek Revival Style buildings, and the town hall, a solid brick structure built in the Romanesque Revival style with a crenelated tower. Other buildings of note include the United Church of Winchester, Conant Public Library, and the Alexander homestead (Eleanor Lambert Murphy Memorial Community Center).

Another nearby attraction is the Chesterfield Gorge Area, with picnic tables, grills, rest rooms, information center, and a 0.7-mile loop trail leading to falls and cascades through Chesterfield Gorge. From Keene, go 5.5 miles west on Route 9. Open weekends from Memorial Day, daily June mid-Oct.

27

Honey Hill

Rating: Easy to moderate. A woodland walk past stone walls, wildflowers and thickets of mountain laurel, toward a bald-faced ledge with good views of hills around Keene Valley and Mount Monadnock.
Distance: 2.25 miles
Hiking time: 1.5 hours
Lowest Elevation: 480 feet
Highest Elevation: 860 feet
USGS Map: Winchester
Other Maps: Swanzey Conservation Commission Map

An ideal family outing is along the trail leading to the top of Honey Hill, where you'll enjoy bursts of color and views of Mount Monadnock rising beyond the shoreline of Dublin Lake. Located in Swanzey, Honey Hill is a property protected through conservation easements and the Land Conservation Investment Program (LCIP) and monitored by the Swanzey Conservation Commission. Although it remains private land, the public is invited to use the blue-blazed trail that leads from Route 32 to the summit.

Access: To reach the trailhead from Manchester, take Route 101 to Route 12 in Keene. Continue on Route 12 south for 0.9 mile to Route 32 (Old Homestead Highway). Continue 4.9 miles on Route 32 south, past Swanzey Center, to a metal gate on the east side of the road near a pasture. Park on the shoulder of the road opposite a green-shuttered white farm house. Do not block gate. Walk south for 0.15 mile on Route 32, using caution. Look for the entrance to a field on the right. Continue walking across the field for 175 yards.

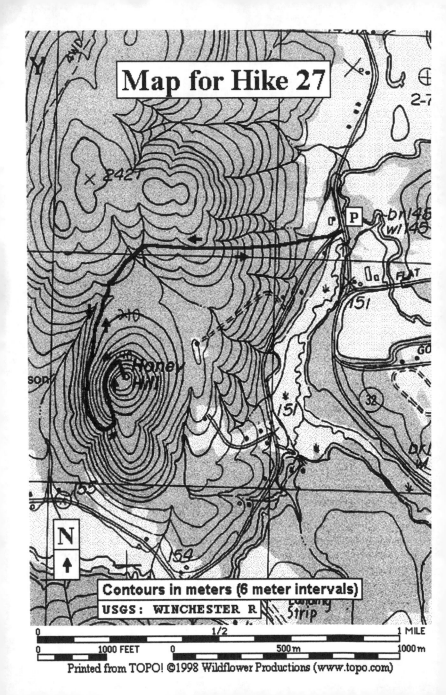

Map for Hike 27

Contours in meters (6 meter intervals)

USGS: WINCHESTER R

N

Printed from TOPO! ©1998 Wildflower Productions (www.topo.com)

Description: The blue-blazed trail leads uphill on a woods road through a mixed forest of oak, pine, hemlock, beech, birch and maple. After five minutes walk, bear left at a fork and continue uphill following the blue blazes. Along the path are clubmosses, ferns, wild sarsaparilla and wintergreen. In early spring you will find violets, bluets, starflowers and wood anemone. After several more minutes walk, and just past a large boulder on the right, turn left into the woods at the end of a stone wall. There is a wooden pine tree trail marker here. Continue following the blue-blazed trail, now going downhill through a hemlock forest.

After another five minutes, you will cross two wooden plank bridges. After crossing a private woods road, you'll come to a blue-yellow trail junction. Bear left and continue following blue blazes. As the trail levels out, you see an impressive display of mountain laurel, and then on the right, a smooth ledge offering a view to the west of Franklin Mountain (1,422 feet). Further to the south are Bullard Mountain, Rattlesnake Mountain, and the sugarloaf-shaped Gunn Mountain.

Just beyond this outlook, the trail begins to switchback up the mountain. After passing a yellow-blazed spur trail on the right, you come to a good view of Swanzey Lake to the west, with Stratton Mountain (Vermont) in the distance. It's a short scramble from here to the summit, where there is a 180-degree view. To the north is Mount Caesar (See *Mt. Caesar Option* on the next page), and the hills around the Keene valley. In the valley to the east is the village of East Swanzey and a large gravel pit. Beyond these are the Marlborough-Richmond ridge and Mount Monadnock. Retrace your steps to return to your vehicle.

Sightseeing: After your walk, you might like to visit Swanzey, which boasts one of the densest concentrations of covered bridges in the country. A map and directions to the bridges are available at the Swanzey Historical Museum located on Route 10, West Swanzey. (Open Monday-Friday, from 1 to 5 p.m.; weekends and holidays, 10 a.m. to 5 p.m., from mid-May through the foliage season. 603-352-4579)

Swanzey is actually made up of several village centers, including Westport, East Swanzey, North Swanzey, West Swanzey, and Swanzey Center. The Potash Bowl, an open-air natural arena, is located in Swanzey Center, where "The Old Homestead," is performed annually in July, a play based on the lives of 19th-century townspeople (603-352-0697).

You might also wish to visit the old Holbrook Farm, which is believed to be where Joyce Kilmer composed his famous poem, "Trees." The story goes that Kilmer was looking out from the porch of the farmhouse at a panorama of majestic maples and scribbled his verse on a brown paper bag. To get to the site of his inspiration from the trailhead parking area, drive south for 0.3 mile on Route 32 to Swanzey Lake Road. Continue 2.4 miles and turn onto Pebble Hill Road (dirt). Go 0.3 mile to Winch Hill Road. The Holbrook Farm is located 0.4 mile further down Winch Hill Road.

Mt. Caesar Option (45 minutes): You can view the rocky ledges of 962-foot-high Mt. Caesar looming over Swanzey Center as you drive north on Route 32 back toward the village. The mountain was named for Caesar Freeman, a freed Black slave, and it was once used as an Indian lookout. To get to Mt. Caesar, look for the white entrance gate to the Mt. Caesar Cemetery opposite the Swanzey Town Hall. Drive through the entranceway between the stone posts and bear to the right. After 0.1 mile, park near the huge white pine trees.

Thompson covered bridge, West Swanzey

The trail, a woods road bordered to either side by a stone wall, begins just beyond a stone wall in the far corner of the cemetery 200 feet to the right. After moving over a ledgy section, the trail descends and comes to an overgrown stretch of felled stag horn sumac. Just beyond this, a woods road intersects from the right. Continue (left) on this road, walking past fallen trees that cross the path. Ten minutes from the start of the walk, near a residence, the trail forks to the left again. Continue uphill through a hardwood forest. Ten minutes more of walking brings you to the south-facing ledges topped by a red beacon light on a 50-foot metal pole. Just before reaching the top, look to the left to see an interesting glacial erratic. From the ledges, below you to the east lies the village of Swanzey Center. Honey Hill is directly south. The biggest mountain to the west is Franklin Mountain, and sugarloaf-shaped Gunn Mountain is to the left of Franklin.

Enjoying the spectacular views of the Monadnock region

28

Monroe Hill - Fox State Forest

Rating: An easy walk along an old town road and forested path leading to a viewing platform on Monroe Hill with views of Crotched Mountain, Mt. Monadnock and the Contoocook River Valley.
Distance: 1.8 miles
Hiking time: 1 hour
Lowest Elevation: 800 feet
Highest Elevation: 1,210 feet
USGS Map: Hillsborough Upper Village
Other Maps: New Hampshire Department of Resources and Economic Development Map

Located on the fringe of the Monadnock Region, Fox State Forest in Hillsborough is 1,445 acres of undeveloped forest land. 22 miles of trails take you past old cellar holes, cemeteries, bogs, marshes, ponds, old growth beech and hemlock, plus a black gum swamp and a quaking bog.

Fox State Forest began in 1922 as a gift to the state of 348 acres from Caroline A. Fox, whose summer home now serves as the forest headquarters building for the South Region of the Division of Forests and Lands. Nearby is the Henry I. Baldwin Environmental Center which is used for forestry and conservation meetings and environmental education. Trail maps are available at the headquarters. No motorized vehicles are allowed in the Forest.

Access: To reach the trailhead from Keene, take Route 9 north to Hillsborough. From the traffic signal in the center of Hillsborough, drive north on School Street, which changes to Center Road. Fox State Forest is 2 miles further on the right.

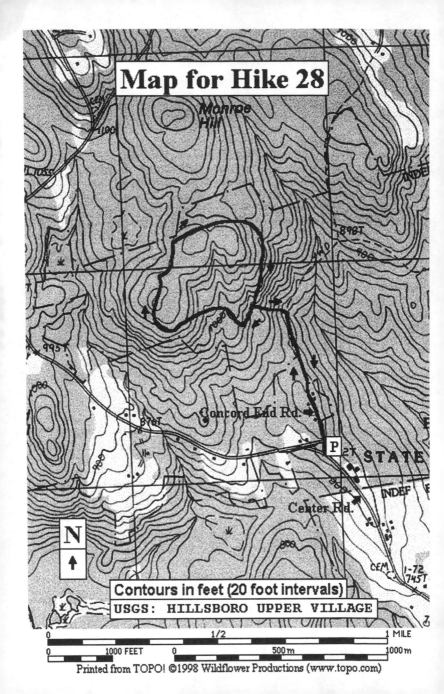

Map for Hike 28

Monroe Hill

Concord End Rd.

P

STATE

Center Rd.

N

Contours in feet (20 foot intervals)

USGS: HILLSBORO UPPER VILLAGE

| 0 | 1/2 | 1 MILE |
| 0 | 1000 FEET | 0 | 500 m | 1000 m |

Printed from TOPO! ©1998 Wildflower Productions (www.topo.com)

Description: Walk north past the large dirt parking lot. The hike starts on Concord End Road (dirt). After five minutes, you will pass a sign pointing the way (left) to Spring Road. 200 yards further, you come to the Gerry Cemetery on the right. Less than a quarter mile still further, you reach an old cellar hole on the left.

All along, the road you've walked has been bordered by stone walls. Weather-etched, lichen-covered, and colored an ageless grey, New Hampshire stone walls were built from the granite rubble left by melting glaciers. There is evidence that some of these walls or similar structures were already here prior to the Anglo-European invasions of the seventeenth century, but most of the history books tell us the story of the hard-toiling settlers who used the stones to enclose pastures and mark property boundaries. Reminders of the days when farms and pastures were everywhere, these dignified symbols of old New England were built "horse-high, hog-tight, and bull-strong."

The pace of the walk quickens as the trail moves uphill. At the top of the rise, turn left onto Spring Road. In 150 yards, a sign designates the way (right) to the Ridge Trail. At this point the trail blazes are marked in red and white. You'll continue walking uphill through a hemlock forest and past large boulders. After stepping through a gap in a stone wall for a second time, you'll walk past a grove of beech trees.

Beech trees are sometimes called "money trees." This is because you can scrunch up one of the ellipse-shaped leaves and it will unfold to its original shape when you release your grip, much like a dollar bill does. Look for beech trees with claw scratches and broken upper branches -- signs that tell you Mr. Bear (Ursus americanus) has been around.

Beechnuts provide an important food source for black bears in October, supplementing their omnivorous diet of squirrels, birds, eggs, fish, frogs, ants and their larvae, young bees, honey, and berries. A bear will find a comfortable seat in the crotch of a beech tree in order to reach out and pull back the limbs to strip the nuts. Don't worry -- there's little chance you'll come upon a black bear, as this large forest dweller usually likes his own company best. If you do encounter a bear in a tree, he's likely to stay put. Bears learn to climb as a way to escape and hide from predators, not as a means of pouncing on prey or people.

Beyond the beech grove, the trail winds gradually uphill. In five minutes you'll reach the platform lookout in a clearing. Stop here for a view to the southwest of Crotched Mountain, Pack Monadnock Mountain and Mount Monadnock. The twin summits of Riley and Gibson Mountains in Antrim rise in the foreground.

The Ridge Trail drops away from the tower to the southwest. Your route continues north on the Monroe Hill Trail, which is marked by white blazes. After a few minutes, you'll reach the Ridge Trail junction where a turn to the left would lead west to Molly J. Road. Instead, continue straight ahead (north) on the Ridge Trail. The white blazes will change to red and white as the trail continues downhill past hemlock trees and a boggy area. After crossing a stone culvert, the trail opens up into a woods road. Several minutes of walking brings you to the Spring Road junction. Continuing downhill on Spring Road brings you past a spring house on the right.

You start to see white birch and quaking (trembling) aspen, which are known as pioneer trees because they rapidly seed in after a timber disturbance. In this area, the disturbance was the Hurricane of 1938 which destroyed over one-million board feet of timber in Fox State Forest alone.

Although aspen and white birch thrive in open areas with abundant light, they cannot compete with more shade-tolerant species such as oak, white pine and hemlock which reach greater heights and overshadow them. By the time the more timber-valued species are able to thrive, the aspens and white birch have come to maturity and declined.

Continuing along the trail, a few minutes walk from the spring house brings you back to the Ridge Trail junction. Turn left and walk back to the parking lot. This route is only one of many possibilities in Fox State Forest. Another popular route leads to Mud Pond, a quaking bog, in the eastern part of the forest. There are also "tree identification" and "mushroom identification" trails to explore.

Sightseeing: You can visit the Franklin Pierce Homestead historic site (his boyhood home), located three miles west of Hillsborough near the junction of Routes 9 and 31. The Hillsborough Historical Society maintains and staffs this old (1804) colonial house, which is open for tours every day in July and August, weekends in June and September through Columbus Day. To get to the Pierce homestead from the center of Hillsborough, drive west 1.4 miles on Route 9 to its junction with Route 202. Continue on Route 9 west for 1.6 miles to Route 31. The Homestead is located 0.1 mile north on Route 31. For information, call 603-478-3165.

You may want to visit nearby Gleason Falls, where there is picnicking, wading and fishing. Also nearby is the site of one of the town's first grist mills. Built between 1830 and 1860 by Scotch-Irish masons who used rough, locally-hewn granite, three of the town's stone arch bridges are in active use. To get to Gleason Falls from the junction of Routes 9 and 202, drive west for 0.3 mile on Route 9 and turn onto Beard Road. After 1.7 miles, Beard Road, turns to dirt (a sign reads "passenger cars only"). Go another 1.1 mile on Beard Rd. En route you will notice a double arch stone bridge on your right.

Concord End Road, Fox State Forest

29

Marlboro Trail - Mount Monadnock

Rating: Strenuous. Trail climbs the western slope of Mount Monadnock over open ledges with numerous overlooks. Some stretches of ledge will be too steep for younger children.
Distance: 4.2 miles
Hiking time: 3 hours
Lowest Elevation: 1,325 feet
Highest Elevation: 3,165 feet
USGS Map: Monadnock
Other Maps: New Hampshire Division of Parks & Recreation Map, AMC Guidebook Map, SPNHF Monadnock-Sunapee Greenway Trailguide, New England Cartographics Map, AMC Metacomet-Monadnock Trail Guide.

One of the oldest trails (at least 150 years old), the Marlboro Trail offers good views and geological sights along the way, as well as alpine flowers and a rock house for children to explore. This route climbs steadily, so be prepared for a workout. If you've never hiked Mount Monadnock, you might want to start with the relatively easy White Dot or White Cross Trail. This route climbs the western slope of Mount Monadnock over open ledges to the stark alpine beauty of the summit cone.

Access: From the Manchester area, take Route 101 west to Milford and on to Route 202 West in Peterborough. Continue for 6.3 miles, then take Route 124 west for 7.4 miles to Shaker Road (2.1 miles beyond the Old Toll Road entrance to Monadnock). Follow Shaker Road (dirt) for 0.7 mile and park near an old cellar hole and clearing on the left. The trailhead begins opposite the parking area on land owned by the Society for Protection of New Hampshire Forests.

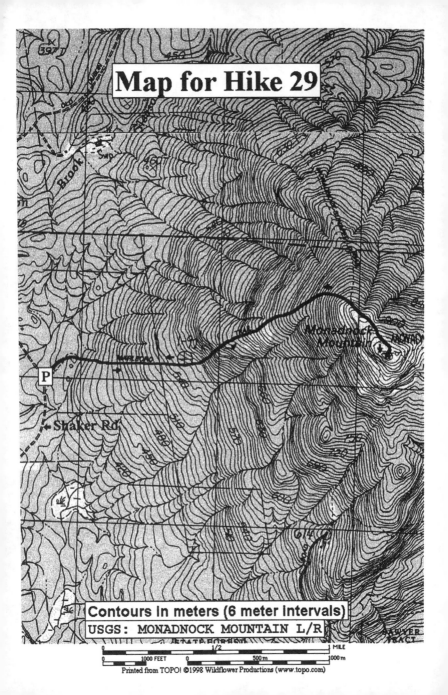

Map for Hike 29

Brook
Swp.

Monadnock
Mountain

MONAD

P

Shaker Rd

Contours in meters (6 meter Intervals)
USGS: MONADNOCK MOUNTAIN L/R

| 0 | | 1/2 | | MILE |
| 0 | 1000 FEET | 0 | 500 m | 1000 m |

Printed from TOPO! ©1998 Wildflower Productions (www.topo.com)

Description: The white-blazed trail goes through a Northern hardwood forest of sugar maple, birch, oak, beech, white pine and hemlock. The rocky path climbs steadily uphill and crosses a stone wall after 15 minutes of hiking. Ten minutes of rugged climbing puts you on an open ledge with good views to the south and west of Troy, Perkins Pond, Gap and Little Monadnock Mountains. Just ahead on the trail is another open ledge with even wider views. Here you'll see Monta Rosa, a minor peak (2,540 feet) on Monadnock's southwest shoulder, and the prominent false summit of Dublin Peak (3,060 feet).

For the next ten minutes, the trail moves through hardwood, spruce, and ledge outcrops. It is possible to experience several different ecological zones on Monadnock, changes which are due to the mountain's exposure to weather. As the trail rises, the maples and beech disappear, the woods become wetter, and you'll notice an increase in weather-stunted spruce which become shorter and more gnarled, their tops bent from the prevailing northwest winds. One mile into the hike, you emerge at a wide open ledge marked by several cairns and white markers. This outcrop makes an ideal spot to rest and explore the rock house. Good views of Stratton Mountain and other Vermont ski peaks can be seen to the northwest. The Marian trail leads to the south (right) from here.

As you continue on the trail, you see Mount Ascutney to the northwest, a mountain almost exactly paired in height with Monadnock at 3,168 feet. The trail continues through alternating ledges and woods for another twenty minutes and then you reach the treeline. A final scramble brings you to the ledges just below the summit.

At the summit of Mount Monadnock

Above the treeline it is easy to see the seven quartzite folds in the mountain. A good deal of Monadnock consists of metamorphic rock called schist, which is inter-layered with light gray quartzite. Continuing along the trail, the Dublin Trail enters from the left (north). The Dublin Trail is the Monadnock-Sunapee (Greenway) Trail. From here the joint trail continues another 0.3 mile to the summit and Mount Monadnock's famous six-state view.

The alpine vegetation at the top includes sandwort and three-leafed cinquefoil, delicate plants which form mats and have five-petaled white flowers that bloom June to August. These hardy little plants thrive in the harshest and most wind-blown terrain, and they are usually found only on the higher peaks of the White Mountains. Be sure to stay on marked trails or bare rock above treeline because these mountain flora are fragile and cannot survive trampling.

Stunted red spruce and balsam fir grow in the bare soil of the exposed summit and pools of rainwater form on the rocky plateau. Lichens are the best adapted organisms in the alpine zone as they require no soil to grow. You'll also find sheep laurel, mountain cranberry (lingonberry), mountain holly, three-forked rushes, blueberries, mountain ash, Rhodora, chokeberry, and withe bushes growing in sheltered areas. After you've enjoyed exploring the summit, retrace your path to return to your vehicle.

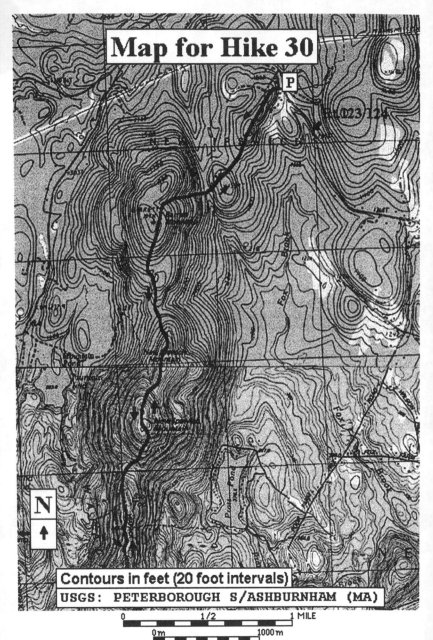

Map for Hike 30

P

Rd 023/124

Contours in feet (20 foot intervals)

USGS: PETERBOROUGH S/ASHBURNHAM (MA)

N

0   1/2   1 MILE

0 m   1000 m

Printed from TOPO! ©1998 Wildflower Productions (www.topo.com)

30

Stony Top - New Ipswich Mountain

Rating: Moderate with short, difficult stretches. This hike features historic roads, stone walls, pond, and spruce and hemlock forests. It follows the Wapack Trail to Stony Top, a ledge outcrop with views of Mount Monadnock and the Souhegan and Contoocook River Valleys.
Distance: 7.6 miles (optional extension 9.1 miles)
Hiking time: 3.5 hours (optional extension 5.5 hours)
Lowest Elevation: 1,440 feet
Highest Elevation: 1,881 feet
USGS Map: Ashburnham, Peterborough South
Other Maps: Wapack Trail Guide Map

The yellow-blazed 21-mile-long Wapack Trail follows a chain of monadnocks running from Mount Watatic in Ashburnham on the Massachusetts border to North Pack Monadnock Mountain in Greenfield, New Hampshire. This moderate hike, with its short difficult stretches, leads to Stony Top, a ledge outcrop just south of New Ipswich Mountain. There are opportunities for blueberry picking, and there's a good chance that you'll flush a ruffed grouse, startle a deer, or see turkey vultures soaring the thermals. This is one of the more heavily wooded sections of the Wapack Trail, but there are also numerous lookout points. An optional longer hike carries you further south to the terminus of the Wapack Trail at the Massachusetts 119 parking lot in Ashburnham, but this requires spotting cars.

Access: Starting at the junction of Routes 101 and 202 in Peterborough, follow Route 202 west to Jaffrey, then Route 124 east for 6.6 miles to the junction of Routes 123/124 (Turnpike Road). Continue south on 123/124 for 0.6 mile to the site of the old Wapack Lodge which was struck by lightning and burned in the summer of 1993. Look for a sign that says "Wapack Road" (dead end), a private dirt drive on the right. Park on the road shoulder or at a cleared dirt parking lot off Old Rindge Road opposite the lodge site. The trailhead begins twenty yards from the old Wapack Lodge.

To reach the trailhead from Manchester, take Route 101 west to Milford, then Route 101 west to Route 31 South in Wilton. Continue on Route 31 for 9.3 miles, then take Route 124 West (it joins Route 123 to become 123/124) for 7.7 miles to the site of the old Wapack Lodge.

Description: The yellow-blazed trail begins with climbing an embankment, then moves through a mixture of oak, maple, spruce, birch and pine. Near the top of the incline, a bulletin board displays a map of the entire Wapack Trail. After passing a residence on the right and stepping through a gap in the stone wall, the trail widens and moves downhill through tall spruce trees and several intersecting ski trails. Use caution as the trail crosses several ski trails for more than a mile through the Windblown Ski Touring Center. Shortly, a Wapack sign directs you to the left. You climb uphill past ferns to a ledge outcrop looking south to Watatic Mountain. Barrett and New Ipswich Mountains are also visible.

After working your way down the ledge and stepping through a gap in a stone wall, the trail levels out, then turns left again. Continue past several more ski trails, turning left two more times, then descend into a hollow.

After crossing a road, the trail turns right to climb the rugged eastern slope of Barrett Mountain for the first steep portion of the hike. A seasonal brook parallels the trail here and there are large boulders and stout birch and beech trees rooted in the mountainside. The trail continues uphill, crosses another road, then levels out on Barrett's north shoulder at an old pasture marked with juniper, birch, steeplebush and meadowsweet.

Along the trail to Stony Top

Another sign, "To Mt. Watatic -- Wapack," directs you to the right. There are limited views as the trail passes over Barrett Mountain and enters a dense spruce forest. In the next 0.7 mile, you will cross stone walls, descend into shaded hollows, and climb two minor knobs. Eventually you reach a ledge affording a good view of Temple and Pack Monadnock Mountains to the north, as well as Kidder Mountain to your right and Mount Monadnock to the west.

The trail continues back into woods with occasional ledges and views to the west of Mount Monadnock, Little Monadnock and Gap mountains. After fifteen minutes you reach another ledge with a wider view of the same mountains. Three more minutes of walking brings you to the actual summit of New Ipswich Mountain which is wooded with no view. Another 15 minutes walking south brings you to Stony Top, a major clearing with wide views toward Mount Monadnock.

To get to Stony Top from the summit of New Ipswich Mountain, continue on the trail which descends into quiet woods and crosses two stone walls before emerging at a ledge area overgrown with juniper, blueberries and oak. Here you'll get a good view of Pratt, Watatic and Wachusett Mountains. From the ledge area, the trail then drops into a gap, moves past the Pratt Pond Trail (blue-blazed on the left), and a brook before rising to Stony Top. Enjoy the views here before making your return trip.

Optional Extension: Leave one vehicle at the Mass 119 parking lot in Ashburnham, Massachusetts, and a second car off Route 123/124 near the old Wapack Lodge in New Ipswich. Follow the trail directions outlined above until you reach Stony Top, where the Wapack Trail offers spectacular views in all directions. To the west, you can see the second Meeting House in Rindge Center, one of the largest buildings of its kind in northern New England.

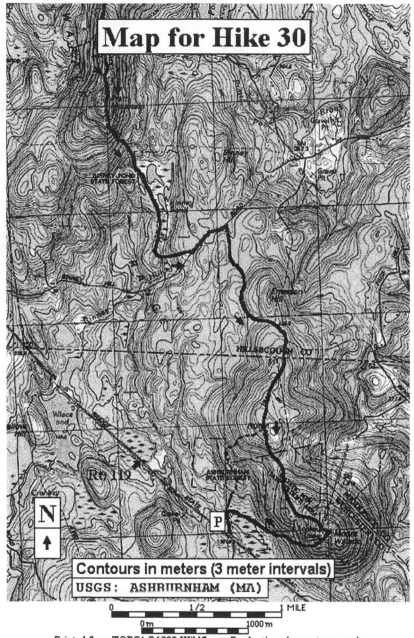

Map for Hike 30

Contours in meters (3 meter intervals)

USGS: ASHBURNHAM (MA)

Rt. 119

HILLSBOROUGH CO

N

P

0   1/2   1 MILE

0 m   1000 m

Printed from TOPO! ©1998 Wildflower Productions (www.topo.com)

From Stony Top, follow the Wapack Trail over the top of wooded Pratt Mountain. The trail descends to move past the western edge of Binney Pond, then turns left to follow Binney Hill Road. It then turns right (south) to follow a logging road to the Massachusetts state line, passes over Nutting Hill (1,620 feet), and moves on to the summit of Mount Watatic (See **Hike #20**). From Watatic's summit, the Wapack Trail heads southwest and descends to the Mass 119 parking lot. If you wish to avoid the summit of Mount Watatic, just after you cross the Massachusetts border, a connector branches right to the Mid-State and State Line Trail which continue 1.25 mile to the Mass 119 parking lot.

Sightseeing: After you complete your hike, you may wish to visit the Nussdorfer Nature Area, a 60-acre nature preserve located in New Ipswich off Route 124, 2.2 miles from the junction of Routes 31 and 124, and 0.5 mile east of Mascenic Regional High School. Also located off of Route 124 is the Rhoads Easement with two miles of loop trails, the yellow-blazed Furnace Brook and Island Trails on the Souhegan River. One end of the trails is on Mill Street behind Warwick Mills. Mill Street is located 0.1 mile south of the junction of Routes 123 and 124. Parking is available for several cars.

Key to USGS Maps

Hike #		USGS Map
1	Shieling Forest	Peterborough North
2	Kidder Mountain	Peterborough South
3	Ponemah Bog	South Merrimack
4	The Heald Tract	Greenville
5	Pitcher Mountain	Stoddard
6	Temple Mountain North	Peterborough South
7	Temple Mountain South	Peterborough South
8	Little Monadnock Mountain	Monadnock
9	Skatutakee Mountain	Marlborough
10	Bald Mountain	Stoddard
11	North Pack Monadnock	Greenfield
12	Pack Monadnock Mountain	Peterborough South
13	Greenfield - French Roads	Greenfield
14	Joe English Reservation	Pinardville
15	Purgatory Falls	New Boston
16	Bald Rock - Mt. Monadnock	Monadnock
17	Crotched Mountain	Peterborough North
		Greenfield
18	Edward MacDowell Lake	Peterborough North
		Marlborough
19	Gap Mountain	Monadnock
20	Mount Watatic	Ashburnham (Mass.)
21	Goose Pond	Keene
22	Hyland Hill	Keene
23	Sucker Brk. Cove - Silver Lk.	Marlborough
24	Meetinghouse Pond	Marlborough
25	Betsy Fosket Sanctuary	Peterborough South
26	Kilburn Pond	Winchester
27	Honey Hill	Winchester
28	Monroe Hill-Fox State Forest	Hillsborough
29	Marlboro Tr., Mt. Monadnock	Monadnock
30A	Stony Top - New Ipswich	Peterborough South,
30B		Ashburnham (Mass.)

References

Appalachian Mountain Club. *AMC White Mountain Guide.*
Boston: Appalachian Mountain Club, 26th edition, 1998.

Baldwin, Henry I. *Monadnock Guide,* 4th ed.
Concord, NH: Society for the Protection of New Hampshire Forests, 1987.

Day, Freida C. *Historic Mont Vernon, Vol. I.*
Mont Vernon New Hampshire Historical Society, 1990.

Day, Freida C. *Mont Vernon Hotels: The Golden Days.*
Mont Vernon New Hampshire Historical Society, 1994.

Doan, Daniel. *Fifty More Hikes in New Hampshire.*
Countryman Press, 1998.

Flanders, John E. *Wapack Trail Guide.*
West Peterborough, NH: Friends of the Wapack, 1993.

Jorgensen, Neil. *A Guide to New England's Landscape.*
Chester, CT: Pequot Press, 1977.

Kibling, Mary L. *Walks and Rambles in the Upper Connecticut Valley.* Woodstock, VT: Backcountry Publications, 1989.

Lindemann, Bob, and Mary Deaett. *Fifty Hikes in Vermont.*
5th ed. Green Mountain Club, 1997.

Tanner, Ogden. *New England Wilds.*
New York: Time-Life Books, 1974.

Thompson, Betty Flanders. *The Changing Face of New England.* New York: The MacMillan Co., 1958.

Whittemore, Suzanne. *In the Shadow of Monadnock.*
Keene, N.H: Historical Society of Cheshire County, 1993.

Workers of the Federal Writers' Project, Works Progress Administration for the State of New Hampshire. *New Hampshire : A Guide to the Granite State.*
Cambridge, MA: The Riverside Press, 1938.

Local Conservation Commissions

Alstead Conservation Committee
Town Hall, PO Box 65, Alstead NH 03602   (603-835-2242)

Amherst Conservation Commission
PO Box 960, Amherst NH 03031   (603-673-6041)

Bennington Conservation Commission
Town Hall, 7 School Street, Unit 101, Bennington NH 03442
(603-588-2189)

Brookline Conservation Committee
PO Box 360, Bond Street, Brookline NH 03033   (603-673-8933)

Charlestown Conservation Commission
Selectmen's Office, PO Box 385, Charlestown NH 03603
(603-826-5821)

Chesterfield Conservation Commission
504 Route 63, Box 175, Town Offices, Chesterfield NH 03443
(603-363-8071)

Fitzwilliam Conservation Commission
Town Hall, Fitzwilliam Common, Fitzwilliam NH 03447
(603-585-7723)

Greenville Conservation Commission
PO Box 343, 46 Main St., Greenville NH 03048   (603-878-4155)

Harrisville Conservation Commission
Town Hall, PO Box 34, Harrisville NH 03450   (603-827-5546)

Hillsborough Conservation Commission
Town Hall, PO Box 7, Hillsborough NH 03244   (603-464-5571)

Hollis Conservation Commission
Town Hall, 7 Monument Square, Hollis NH 03049   (603-465-2064)

Jaffrey Conservation Commission
Town Offices, 10 Goodnow St., Jaffrey NH 03452   (603-532-7861)

Lyndeborough Conservation Commission
Citizens' Hall, Lyndeborough NH 03082   (603-654-9653)

Marlborough Conservation Commission
PO Box 487, Marlborough NH 03455 (603-876-4529)

Marlow Conservation Commission
Town Offices, Marlow NH 03456 (603-446-2245)

Mason Conservation Commission
Mann House, Darling Road, Mason NH 03048 (603-878-2070)

Milford Conservation Commission
1 Union Square, Milford NH 03055 (603-673-7964)

Mont Vernon Conservation Commission
Town Offices, Main St., PO Box 44, Mont Vernon NH 03057
(603-673-9126)

New Hampshire Association of Conservation Commissions
54 Portsmouth St., Concord NH 03301 (603-224-7867)

New Ipswich Conservation Commission
30 Triknit Road, New Ipswich NH 03071 (603-878-2772)

Peterborough Conservation Commission
1 Grove St., Towne House, Peterborough NH 03458 (603-924-8010)

Rindge Conservation Commission
Rindge Town Offices, Payson Hill Road, Rindge NH 03461
(603-899-5181)

Swanzey Conservation Commission
PO Box 9, East Swansey NH 03446 (603-352-7411)

Walpole Conservation Commission
Town Hall, Elm St., PO Box 729, Walpole NH 03608 (603-756-3514)

Weare Conservation Commission
PO Box 190, Weare NH 03281 (603-529-7575)

Wilton Conservation Commission
PO Box 83, Wilton NH 03086 (603-654-9451)

Winchester Conservation Commission
Town Hall, PO Box 25, Winchester NH 03470 (603-239-4951)

Local Nonprofit Conservation and Recreation Organizations

The American Hiking Society
1422 Fenwick Lane, Silver Spring MD 20910   (301-565-6704)
www.americanhiking.org

Amherst Land Trust
P.O. Box 753, Amherst NH 03031

Appalachian Mountain Club
5 Joy Street, Boston MA 02108   (617-523-0636)
New Hampshire Chapter, 97 Worthly Rd., Bedford NH 03110

Audubon Society of New Hampshire
3 Silk Farm Road, Concord NH 03301-8200   (603-224-9909)

Beaver Brook Association
117 Ridge Road, Hollis NH 03049 (603-465-7787)

Department of Resources and Economic Development
Bureau of Trails
Box 1856, Concord NH 03302-1856   (603-271-3254)

Friends of the Wapack
PO Box 115, West Peterborough NH 03468

Harris Center for Conservation Education
King's Highway, Hancock NH 03449   (603-525-3394)

Harris Center/Senior Focus
Outdoor Walkers
(603-924-6090)

Milford Outing Club
Town Hall, Milford NH 03055   (603-673-3403)

Monadnock Audubon Society
(603-352-WILD)

Monadnock Conservancy
P.O.Box 337, Keene NH 03431-0337   (603-357-0600)

Monadnock Sierra Club
P.O. Box 1351, Keene NH 03431   (603-357-2239)

Monadnock Travel Council
48 Central Square, Keene NH 03431   (603-352-1308; 800-432-7864)

Monadnock Sunapee Greenway Trail Club
PO Box 164, Marlow NH 03456

The Nature Conservancy, New Hampshire Chapter
2-1/2 Beacon St., Suite 6, Concord NH 03301-4447   (603-224-5853)

New Hampshire Sierra Club
3 Bicentennial Square, Concord NH 03301   (603-224-8222)
www.sierraclub.org/chapters/NH

Society for the Protection of New Hampshire Forests
(SPNHF) 54 Portsmouth Street, Concord NH 03301   (603-224-9945)

Trailwrights
PO Box 785, Hillsborough NH 03244

Products from New England Cartographics

www.necartographics.com

Maps

Holyoke Range State Park (Eastern Section)	$3.95
Holyoke Range/Skinner State Park (Western Section)	$3.95
Mt. Greylock Reservation Trail Map	$3.95
Mt. Toby Reservation Trail Map	$3.95
Mt. Tom Reservation Trail Map	$3.95
Mt. Wachusett and Leominster State Forest Trail Map	$3.95
Western Massachusetts Trail Map Pack	$15.95
(includes all 6 maps listed above)	
Quabbin Reservation Guide	$4.95
Quabbin Reservation Guide (waterproof)	$5.95
New England Trails (general locator map)	$2.95
Grand Monadnock Trail Map	$3.95
Wapack Trail Map	$3.95
Connecticut River Map (in Massachusetts)	$5.95

Books

Guide to the Metacomet-Monadnock Trail (1999)	$8.95
Hiking the Pioneer Valley	$10.95
Skiing the Pioneer Valley	$10.95
Bicycling the Pioneer Valley (1998)	$10.95
High Peaks of the Northeast	$12.95
Steep Creeks of New England (1999)	$14.95
24 Great Rail-Trails of New Jersey (1999)	$16.95
Golfing in New England	$16.95
Hiking Green Mountain National Forest (2000)	$14.95
Hiking the Monadnock Region (2000)	$12.95

Postage/Handling Charges: When ordering by mail, please include $.75 P/H for the first single map and $.25 P/H for each additional map. Include $1.00 for the Western Mass. Map Pack. For any of the books, include $2.00 P/H and $.75 for each additional book, or call for information.

Send for ordering information and current prices to:

New England Cartographics, Inc.
PO Box 9369, North Amherst, MA 01059.
Telephone orders: (413) 549-4124

ORDER FORM

To order, call or write:

New England Cartographics
PO Box 9369
North Amherst, MA 01059
413-549-4124
FAX Orders: 413-549-3621
www.necartographics.com
E-mail: geolopes@crocker.com

Circle one: **Master Card   Visa   Amex   Check**

Card # _____

Expiration Date _____

Signature _____

Telephone (optional) _____

Please send my order to:

Name_____

Street_____

_____

Town/City_____

State_____ **Zip**_____